JUST JUNK

JUST JUNK

NEW LOOKS FOR OLD FURNITURE

Linda Barker

Reader's Digest

READER'S DIGEST ASSOCIATION INC.
Pleasantville, New York / Montreal

A READER'S DIGEST BOOK

Edited and produced by David & Charles
Book design by Jane Forster
Styled photography by Lucinda Symons
Step-by-step photography by Shona Wood

Library of Congress Cataloging in Publication Data

Barker, Linda.
    Just junk : new looks for old furniture / by Linda Barker.
        p.   cm.
    Includes index.
    ISBN 0-7621-0017-6 (pbk.)   ISBN 0-7621-0069-9 (hc)
    1. Furniture—Repairing.   2. Furniture finishing.   I. Title.
TT199.B35 1998
684.1'0028'8—dc21   97-31685

Printed in Italy

CONTENTS

THE LIVING ROOM 29

THE KITCHEN 83

THE DINING ROOM 57

THE BEDROOM 111

INTRODUCTION

You don't need to be a designer to spot a bargain, and there are plenty of places to pick up real junk finds. All the pieces of furniture used in this book were uncovered in yard sales, secondhand stores, thrift stores and attics – with the exception of the dresser, which was about to be thrown away.

This book has been wonderful to work on in many ways. First, it has been a great challenge to make something out of what was basically very ugly, tacky, and unwanted. The "before" photographs are testimony to the disastrous pieces of furniture that found their way into my workroom. It has also been stimulating to work with many different media on basic pieces of furniture. When you are considering decorating a piece of furniture, it is easy to think purely in terms of paint and various paint effects. With this book I hope to have opened up many more possibilities, such as decorating with fabric, photocopies, and metal, in addition to using a range of techniques such as stamping and decoupage.

When faced with the variety of projects in this book, it can be difficult to know where to start with your own junk finds. However, all the decorating techniques are adaptable, and I hope that you will be able to find a treatment to suit your particular find. There certainly is a great deal of fun to be had from rescuing your own junk furniture. Enjoy the time you spend in junk stores and yard sales, and don't be afraid to rummage around. What's more, don't forget to haggle over the price to strike the best bargain – it's all part of the fun!

Take inspiration from our "before" photographs, and remember that even if you only manage to unearth an encrusted, plastic-covered cabinet, you can transform it into something fantastic!

Linda Barker

BUYING JUNK FURNITURE

First, thoroughly check your chosen item of junk before parting with any cash; the thrill of finding a bargain dresser will soon fade if you get it home only to discover that the woodworm was there before you. No matter how cheap the junk is, turn it over, look at the back, look inside, and even look underneath if possible. Check carefully for loose joints, warped drawers or table tops, and blistered veneer. If you still think you can restore it, then buy it.

Practice your bargaining skills before you open your wallet. Always give the impression that the furniture "isn't that great," and that you could either "take it or leave it," even though in reality your heart is pounding at your good fortune of finding the most perfect piece of junk. Generally, most serious traders will meet you halfway on any price negotiations, so don't be afraid to try.

The only items I seriously will not consider buying are those infested with woodworm. Although there are treatments available for the destruction of these little beasts, I have never felt that a piece of junk was really worth the effort. Of course, there may be a time when the junk find is too wonderful a discovery to resist, despite woodworm. It's just that I've never faced that problem yet.

Blistered veneer is another casualty that I tend to steer clear of, although if the piece is worth it, glue can be injected into the blister and pressed flat. Several heavy weights positioned over the drying glue should hold the veneer down until the surface is completely smooth again. Tiny spots of blistered veneer can sometimes be disguised with a clever paint finish or applied decoration, so there are some occasions when the problem can be resolved by a bit of cheating.

Once the handles were removed (below), this simply proportioned cabinet was decorated with a stenciled design (left).

WHERE TO SHOP FOR JUNK

Thrift stores are often worth a quick browse if you're walking past. These places have occasionally turned up a bargain for me, usually the smaller items, such as a bathroom cabinet and the odd kitchen chair. More favorite hunting grounds are well-organized yard sales or garage sales. Check your local papers for details of these events and go with plenty of money, just in case it's a strictly "cash only" occasion. It's very rare that I come away from a yard sale without finding some bargain.

Friends have told me of wonderful European equivalents to the yard sale. The summertime "brocantes" in France are a regular occurrence in small towns and villages, and if you're on vacation in this part of the world and can get things home, then why not make the most of the opportunity?

City street markets are also great places for bargain hunting and are usually held over the weekend. Otherwise, try local salvage yards or auction rooms; sometimes, however, pieces from these places can be quite expensive – more antique prices than junk prices. The traders there can also be somewhat intimidating, but bargains can still be found. It is often those pieces that need more than a quick sanding which are of no real interest to traders, who need to shift their stock quickly. Such items go fairly reasonably, and for those who persevere and wait patiently it is often these pieces that are sold cheaply at the end of an auction.

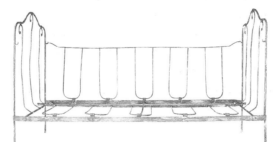

Paint and composition metal leaf instantly transformed two old lamps and a rusty crib.

TOOLS AND MATERIALS

If you walk into any home improvement or interior decorating store, you will see a bewildering choice of materials and equipment available. Don't worry – you do not need everything! In reality, you just need a basic tool kit which will provide you with all the bits and pieces required to tackle most jobs, together with the standard colors of latex paints and a few oil-based paints.

BRUSHES

There is a huge selection of brushes available, and generally you get what you pay for. I choose to work with brushes that will not deposit loose hairs all over my newly painted surface, so I will not buy the cheapest ones. A good basic tool kit should have a selection of the brushes listed below.

Standard bristle brushes in most sizes will equip you for the majority of the projects in this book. Sizes that range from ½ inch (12mm) up to 3 inches (7.5cm) will be quite adequate for most furniture decorating.

Artist's brushes are invaluable for finer detailed work. Both round and flat-headed artist's brushes, in addition to a long-haired fine brush for lining, are useful, as are short, flat-headed stenciling brushes.

BASIC TOOL KIT

Power tools are great, but there is always the equivalent in a hand-powered version. I have to say, however, that I would find life very difficult without a power sander, a power drill, and a power jigsaw, but it depends on the amount of work you are about to undertake. If you get hooked, you will find these tools a worthwhile investment.

Screwdrivers, both Philips head and slotted head, will be needed for practically every job you do. As you build up a tool kit, you will find that it helps to have both a large and small version of each screwdriver, and it is just as well to have a medium size, too.

A good paint scraper is essential, particularly if your penchant is for picking up really heavily painted pieces of junk. Too much paint can deter dealers from buying a piece, as the labor required to strip it cancels out any profit. A wire brush is another useful tool if you plan to strip your junk finds. It can get into tiny cracks and crevices that your scraper blade cannot. An old toothbrush will do in some instances.

A putty knife is essential for smooth filling and repairs; look for a flexible blade and a comfortable handle.

Steel wool and sandpaper are not expensive and are always useful. It is best to have a variety of grades in both cases: coarse, medium, and fine.

Glues are handy to have in a basic tool kit. Craft and wood glue are my stand-bys, while a two-part epoxy glue can be useful for really strong repairs.

Detergent is useful for washing down painted surfaces before painting, if the existing paint is not going to be removed. It removes grease and grime quickly and harshly. Protect your hands when using strong detergents, as its action will be as powerful on your hands as it is on furniture. Be equally careful whenever you use strong chemicals and abrasive materials. Wear gloves at all times, and use a face mask if possible, too. A mask is crucial when sawing composite board as the tiny dust particles are suspected of being carcinogenic. Be warned.

PAINT

The enormous choice of paint colors available can be overwhelming, particularly if your local paint store has a centrifugal color mixer. It is temptation itself to buy every specific color needed for a particular job, whereas, in fact, the most sensible approach

would be to arm yourself with a selection of the universal tints which are sold in most paint stores and make the colors yourself for a fraction of the cost. There has been many an occasion when a color that I have agonized over on a paint chart looks completely different when I've opened the can, and I've often resorted to adding a drop or two of tint in order to achieve the color that I wanted in the first place. Many of the colors used in this book have been mixed using universal tints, with the exception of the darker shades. I buy these colors, such as terra-cotta reds and ultra-deep blues, specifically, but I will add tints to them, too, if the color isn't quite as I expected. Take care using tints with darker colors, though; while tinting lighter colors is both fun and economical, too much tint can upset the balance between the latex medium and the color pigment.

A primer is often used under a paint color as a "key" for the paint to sit on happily. Paint applied directly on a wooden surface may be unstable in some instances and will quickly chip. Primer also protects the wood underneath from the paint above, forming a crucial layer. If you are going to paint a wooden surface with colored paint or glaze,

and the surface is not bare wood, you can use latex primer. If the surface is bare wood however, then oil- or shellac-based primer is better, as latex primer can raise the grain and it can also loosen water-based wood glue in joints.

The paint I use most frequently is latex, and it is the easiest paint to use. Water-based paint, such as latex, dries quickly, and it is very simple to wash brushes, hands, and even faces clean afterward. I avoid using oil (mineral spirit)-based products as much as possible as they are harsh on skin as well as the environment. Provided furniture is well prepared and well protected using primers and varnishes, latex paint will be stable, even on heavily used pieces of furniture. On rare occasions I do use oil-based products, but principally for metal pieces, where latex paint would not work unless a metal primer is used first.

Commercial water-based acrylic glazes are very useful for decorative paint techniques; they dry quickly, are non-yellowing, and are simple to use. Once again, there are oil-based equivalents, but in most cases I favor the water-based glazes for the same reasons that I use latex paint.

Paint finishes can be used to highlight decorative carved detailing like that on this table leg.

VARNISHES

There are two readily available varnishes – polyurethane, which is oil-based, and acrylic, which is water-based. These come in three different finishes – flat, satin, and gloss. Generally speaking, the higher the gloss, the tougher the finish, although all varnishes offer good tough protection against hard knocks and scrapes. Water-based acrylic varnish is the easiest to use since it has a quick drying time and brushes are washed easily in water.

Avoid spray varnishes if at all possible; our planet is a better place without aerosols, and the inhalation of varnish particles can be unavoidable, particularly when you use this product in a small, confined space. Always let one coat of varnish dry completely before applying subsequent layers.

WAX

Furniture wax, the good old-fashioned kind sold in large flat cans and smelling of rich beeswax, is valuable not only for its protective qualities, but also for its effective decorative capabilities. The application of wax over latex paint gives a wonderful patina of age. It darkens the underlying color slightly and smooths the surface, giving it a silky finish. The wax may be applied softly with a cloth, or heavily with steel wool to create a distressed finish.

Wax can be bought in several colors, usually to match specific wood colors, but it is more often available only in a reddish tone of brown, as well as yellow-, medium-, and dark-brown tones, and clear. Always apply wax at the end of the last decorative treatment; it will repel all other products.

OTHER MATERIALS

There are certain specific products you will need for particular projects in this book, such as mylar (acetate sheets) for stenciling, and composition metal leaf used for gilding (see the individual projects). You may not have used these materials before, and it is worth keeping a list of good craft and decorating suppliers upon whom you can call for advice. Thin aluminum sheet, for example, can be difficult to find, but if the punched metal cabinet (see page 104) appeals to your sense of decoration, you'll need to know a supplier. It can be impossible to have all materials on hand when you undertake a project, but knowing where to obtain specific items will save time in the long run.

Craquelure varnish produces a fine network of tiny cracks all over the surface on which it is applied. The effect is highlighted by rubbing a small amount of burnt umber oil color over the dried varnish. The dark oil color is held in the cracks to reveal the crazed appearance. The effect can be used in conjunction with many other decorative paint effects.

BASIC TECHNIQUES AND REPAIRS

The advice provided in this section of the book outlines the unfortunately rather time-consuming, yet fundamental, preparation techniques for getting your piece of furniture ready for its all-important transformation; it is the boring bit, if you like, as opposed to the fun part of decoration. As is the case with many decorating projects, it is this preparation which accounts for all the hard work, and decorating junk furniture is no exception. If you're not opposed to hard work, even the most severely junked piece of furniture – the sort which is found at the back of a thrift store or under a table at the local yard sale – can be given new life.

Rescuing a piece of furniture that is in dire need of repair can be immensely rewarding, but be quite honest with yourself: if the thought of hours spent alone with only your paint stripper and scraper knife for company isn't exactly how you'd like to spend your well-earned weekend off, then perhaps you had better look for something that is in a slightly better condition than "wrecked."

SPECIAL PAINT FINISHES

Once you have completed the preparation, then you can have fun trying some of the many special paint finishes used throughout this book. Antiquing, distressing, color-washing, and gilding can all be used to give your furniture a distinctive touch, and most of them are easy to do. Rather than applying just one coat of latex, for example, why not apply two and distress one through the other? The effect is more pleasing to the eye, and it adds a strong character to a piece of furniture. A simple colorwashed effect is another easy finish and takes no time at all to apply. Colorwashing is rather like scrubbing

paint onto a surface, not like painting at all, but the effect is wonderful.

There is a current fashion for heavily antiqued furniture, using glazes, waxes, or varnish. The simplest way to build a patina of age on a piece of furniture is to apply a colored finishing wax; another method involves distressing the painted surface with a pad of steel wool. These finishes can be used either on their own or combined with other techniques to enhance your furniture.

Many decorative finishes are easy to produce using basic materials and a little know-how. A gold-leaf effect is easy to reproduce using inexpensive composition metal leaf (frame left), while spattering (right), sponging (center), and antiquing (left and above right) can all be created using ordinary household paint.

STRIPPING WOODEN FURNITURE

If your piece of furniture is covered with many layers of old paint or varnish, it may need to be stripped. I sometimes recommend stripping back to the wood underneath because this will give you the best possible surface to work on (but only do so if you are willing to use oil-based products). The quickest and easiest way to do this is to use a commercial paint stripper in liquid or gel form. Let your local hardware store advise you on the right product for your particular piece of furniture since there are many brands on the market. Always follow the advice which will be given to you both by the store and by the manufacturer, whose information will be shown clearly on the label.

Always strip furniture outdoors because the stripper can be noxious and the fumes quite overpowering. Wherever possible, choose an environmentally friendly product and make sure that you dispose of the waste according to the instructions given with the product. Wear strong household gloves and eye protection. **Caution:** *Masks do not protect you from the fumes of methylene chloride, the toxic active ingredient in stripper.*

Hand-stripping furniture in this way is an unpleasant task, but it may be the best method of getting your junk piece back to basics. Occasionally, I have taken items to be commercially dipped in huge tanks, but this is an unforgiving process. The chemicals are immensely strong and will literally strip out any life from the wood. As a result, stripped wood often cracks open, and joints disintegrate completely, particularly if they were previously glued. So, either undertake to strip the furniture yourself, or choose some other decorative finish, such as decoupage, to finish the piece.

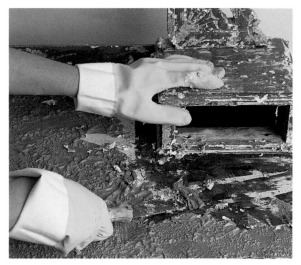

1 Pour a little stripper into a clean, dry glass jar; this is easier than pouring it directly onto the furniture from the can. Dab, rather than brush, a thick film of stripper over the painted surface, working on a small section at a time if the piece of furniture is quite large. Leave the stripper to soak into the painted surface for at least ten minutes, following the manufacturer's specific recommendations.

2 Once the recommended time is up, you will notice that the paint surface has started to blister quite dramatically. The old paint layers can then be stripped away using a stripping knife, by pushing the knife *away* from you. Scrape the old paint into a bag or container that can be disposed of once the job is finished.

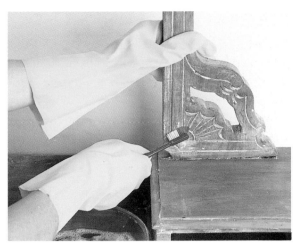

3 Once the thickest part of the paint has been removed, clean off any remaining bits using a pad of medium-grade steel wool soaked in mineral spirits. Rub this reasonably hard into the surface of the piece until the surface is clean. If the pad becomes clogged with paint, turn it over or replace it with a fresh pad.

4 Using a stiff-bristled small brush, brush away any paint deposits in carved details. Brush *away* from yourself, as the bristles may spray a fine mist of stripper and paint which would be dangerous if it came into contact with your face or eyes. Sponge the surface with a soapy cloth to remove any remaining stripper.

5 Let the surface of the wood dry out a little if it still shows damp areas from the stripper. Wrap a piece of fine-grit sandpaper around a block of wood and rub it firmly over the whole surface. This will smooth out any irregularities on the surface of the furniture and remove any small, stubborn bits of paint should there be some still remaining.

6 Wipe the surface with a clean cloth to remove the dust. Paint on a layer of white primer using a thick-bristled household brush. This will seal and protect the wood and provide a good surface for the base color. When the layer of primer is thoroughly dry, rub the surface lightly using a fine-grit sandpaper wrapped around a wooden block, following the grain of the wood, to create an even finish for the base coat. Smaller areas can be sanded without using a block.

PREPARING METAL SURFACES

Occasionally I have uncovered wonderful pieces of junk that are made of metal. Often these pieces are only junked because they are rusty, but as most metalwork is pretty easy to clean up, I regard these finds as a kind of treat. Often the most that is needed to prepare metalwork is a thorough brush-down with a stiff steel brush. The rust will then flake off to reveal shiny metal beneath. Both the chandelier (see page 72) and the day bed (see page 50) were easily prepared in this way before painting. Choose a strong steel brush and rub the metal surface with it until the rust has literally been scrubbed off. With pieces such as the chandelier and day bed, you will find it easier to turn them over, working first on the underside and then on the top. Metal primer is used whenever you apply paint to a metal surface. One coat is usually enough.

1 Scrub the rusty metal surface using a stiff steel brush, brushing away from you to avoid spraying yourself with fragments of rusty metal. Work systematically around the item until all the surface has been treated. Scrub the underneath surface in the same way as the top.

2 Using a narrow paintbrush, apply metal primer over the surface. I use a red metal oxide primer, and it is usually adequate to apply only one coat. Remember to apply the primer underneath the piece as well as on top of it. Drying times will vary, but as the primer is solvent-based, it will certainly need to dry overnight, even if left in a well-ventilated space. (Work outdoors if possible.)

PREPARING FORMICA SURFACES

On the whole, I try to avoid buying formica furniture. Occasionally, however, as the bedroom cabinet shows (see page 112), the furniture may be so appealing that I'll buy it despite its formica top. The primary concern I have with this ultra-smooth, slick surface is that it tries to resist virtually every type of paint applied to it, making it susceptible to every knock and scratch. However, a small area of formica is workable, provided it is "keyed" thoroughly, by scratching it with a saw to create a roughened surface. Wipe the surface with a solution of denatured alcohol to remove any grease.

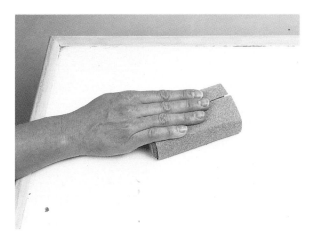

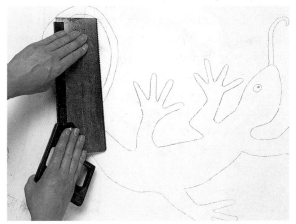

Wipe the surface dry using an absorbent cloth. Wrap medium-grit sandpaper around a wooden block and rub the block in all directions to "key" the plastic surface lightly, ready to receive the paint. Apply a coat of shellac-based paint to the surface; this type of paint will provide the best adhesion. When the first coat has dried, a second coat or a colored glaze coat can be applied if required; sand the first coat lightly before applying the second.

For a formica surface that is to be decorated using mosaic, a more deeply scored surface is required for the tesserae to bond to. The best way of achieving this is to pull the teeth of a small handsaw back and forth over the surface of the formica, quite literally gouging lines deep into the surface. This should be done once the basic outline of the mosaic has been drawn onto the surface as the uneven, scored surface would be difficult to draw on.

REPAIRING HINGES

Often, the only action needed to repair a badly fitting door is to tighten the hinges, which may have become loose with general wear and tear. Hold the door firmly in its correct alignment with one hand and tighten the screws with the other. If screws are damaged or missing, replace them with new brass ones; these should be slightly larger than the old ones so that a stronger bond is made. When choosing a new screw, always check the furniture to see if it can accommodate the screw's length and width.

FILLING CHIPS AND CRACKS

The aim of good preparation is to have the smoothest possible finish on the furniture you are about to embark upon. When dealing with junk furniture, it is unlikely that you will ever find an item that doesn't require some kind of repair, whether it is a small hole that requires filling or a deep gash across a table top.

An all-purpose wood putty solves most problems; it is easy to apply, dries quickly, and can be sanded smooth so that no one would ever suspect the damage underneath. Deeper holes or gashes may need more than one application of putty.

Apply putty to a deep hole using a putty knife, let it dry, then apply a second layer and let it dry. Repeat this procedure until the final layer of putty can be sanded smooth with the surface of the furniture. Use a good putty knife with a flexible blade and, if in doubt, always overfill rather than underfill any imperfections, as the dried putty can always be sanded back to a smooth finish.

Dents on the sides of furniture are better filled using a two-part wood putty, which will dry to a much tougher finish. Your local hardware store should be able to advise you on this type of product.

1 Apply wood putty over the blemish using a putty knife. Push the putty into the hole with the knife, using a downward motion and applying slight pressure on the knife. The aim is to push the putty deep into the gash, where it will bond to the underlying surface. Draw the putty knife slowly across the gash, pulling any excess putty with it. Apply more putty in the same way if necessary. If the hole or gash is very large, apply putty in stages as outlined above.

2 Let the putty dry; it is dry when it has changed to a much lighter color and is hard to the touch. Then sand the surface lightly using fine-grit sandpaper and gently rubbing the surface of the putty in a light circular motion. Once the surface is smooth, wipe away any dust particles with a damp cloth.

FIXING LOOSE JOINTS

Many loose joints on junk furniture are primarily a result of heavy usage. Regluing will often rectify this type of problem quickly, and using modern glues such as cyanoacrylate glue and strong wood glue will mean that the joints stay closed for longer.

When regluing, always use too much rather than too little glue; any excess adhesive can soon be wiped away with a clean cloth. If access to the joint is difficult, use a small stiff-bristled artist's brush to apply glue over the damaged surfaces. After you have applied the glue, clamp the joint to secure the repair until the glue dries; in most cases, you should let glue dry overnight.

1 Open the joints as wide as possible without causing any more harm than is necessary to the piece of furniture. Apply glue to the joints, using the nozzle of the wood glue tube to direct the glue into the joints themselves.

2 Press the two sides together and hold firmly for a few minutes. Wipe excess glue from around the joint with a clean cloth. It may be necessary to tap the joints together lightly using a small hammer. If additional force is needed to bond the two pieces back together, you will need to use a larger hammer, but protect the wood from being dented by it by placing a small block of wood between the hammer and the area that is being repaired.

3 Wherever possible, apply weights or a clamp on top of newly glued joints to keep them secure until the adhesive is firmly set and has dried thoroughly. Often this will mean letting the joints remain like this overnight to make sure of a really good repair that will stand the test of time.

CHANGING A DRAWER KNOB

It may sound basic, but it is surprising how much difference a small drawer knob can make to a piece of furniture. Recently I discovered an entire store devoted solely to knobs! Designers are also beginning to advertise beautiful cabinet pulls, door hardware, and drawer knobs in the classified ads at the back of many design and home interest magazines, so check these pages, too, if you're looking for new ideas.

Remove the old knob from the junk furniture using a screwdriver. If you clean away the dirt and grime that tends to collect around the screw heads on old furniture, you will usually be able to reveal the screw head enough to unscrew the hardware. Rusted-in screws that steadfastly refuse to budge will either need to be cut off with a fretsaw, or sometimes drilled out.

1 Fill the holes that are left after the removal of the old drawer pull using a small amount of wood putty. Push the putty into the holes as you pull the spreader past them, and scrape away any excess from around the sides of the repair. Let the putty dry, then sand lightly to a smooth finish.

2 For a central drawer knob, measure across the width and depth of the drawer to determine the position. Lightly mark the spot with a pencil cross.

3 For a central screwed-on drawer knob, use the pencil mark as a guide for the drill. Put a wood drilling bit on the drill, choosing a bit that is slightly smaller in diameter than the screw itself. Hold the drawer firmly with one hand and drill vertically into the drawer.

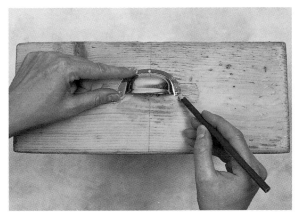

4 Screw the knob into the hole. Sometimes wooden knobs such as this one are purchased with the screw already in place. Other knobs require a screw to be passed through from inside the drawer, through the drilled hole and into the wooden knob.

5 For a drawer handle like this one that takes three screws, position the handle over the center of the drawer, marking the center line if necessary to align the handle correctly. Using a light pencil, mark through the screw-hole positions, remove the handle and use the pencil marks as guides for the drill.

DECORATING A DRAWER KNOB

Wooden knobs are easy to decorate; treat them as you would any blank surface. Choose unfinished wood if at all possible, as it needs no preparation at all. For wood that has been previously lacquered or waxed, simply prepare it as if it were a piece of furniture. Steel wool soaked in a little mineral spirits will remove wax, and sanding will key an ultra-smooth surface such as lacquer. If the knobs are painted, either sand them or use a little paint stripper.

Metal knobs can also be decorated successfully. To create an antique finish on a new brass knob, mix a little burnt umber oil paint with a little polyurethane varnish and stipple the color over the brass surface.

Distressed colors such as bright yellow showing underneath slate blue can be effective on a country-style piece of furniture. For the most effective results when distressing, choose colors that are opposite on the color spectrum, as shown at right.

Decoupage can also be very effective on drawer knobs. Once again, choose a background color that will set off the applied decoupage. Tint the decoupage using watercolors for a softer look; alternatively, a graphic look can be achieved by applying a black and white image onto a dark base color. Glue the decoupaged motif in position, then protect and seal it with at least three layers of acrylic varnish.

REPAIRING A CHAIR

Before buying or rescuing a broken chair such as this one, quickly do a test run to see if the pieces will in fact go back together. This is not as crazy as it may at first seem, as the damage may have occurred as a result of warped wood. If this is the case, the pieces will never fit back squarely, and the chair is best not bought in the first place.

1 Clean the old glue from the base of each spindle and from the holes into which the spindles will fit. Make sure that the spindles fit inside the appropriate holes. Number or label the position of each piece. Squeeze wood glue into the joints and around the spindle bases.

2 Push the separate parts of the chair back together and tap down using a hammer, protecting the wood with a wooden block. Bind the chair back to the base of the chair using strong string, and pull the tension really tight to hold the back in place until the glue has dried.

3 Remove all the old glue from inside the joints and around the spindles of the chair legs. Apply plenty of strong wood glue into the drilled holes and around the ends of the cross-bar and leg sections.

4 Push the chair-leg pieces together and tap in place using a hammer, protecting the wood with a wooden block. When the joints are firmly in place, clamp the frame together to prevent any movement before the glue has dried. The easiest way to do this is to bind twine around the legs, pulling the tension as tight as possible. Leave like this until the glue has set.

REPAIRING MOLDING

Intricate plaster detailing on some picture frames and furniture can become badly damaged with age, and this can often deter prospective buyers. Consequently, I have often seen rather fine examples of plasterwork, particularly picture and mirror frames, stacked away at the back of secondhand stores. This is good news for me, as repairing plaster is not as difficult as it may at first seem. For repairing delicate molded details, look for a specialty two-part putty which is mixed together between your fingers and built up into the missing plasterwork. This is then shaped as required to match the existing plasterwork and sanded if necessary when it is completely dry.

For less ornate details, ordinary wood putty is perfectly adequate. Simply apply it into the missing section. You will find that the putty has enough drying time for you to shape it carefully to match the surrounding plasterwork.

1 Clean around the area to be filled if it looks dusty, and use an old dry toothbrush to get into difficult corners. Using a small modeling tool (readily available from craft stores), press a small dollop of putty into the area to be filled. Press it firmly onto the surface of the bare wood to be sure of a good contact between the wooden surface and the putty.

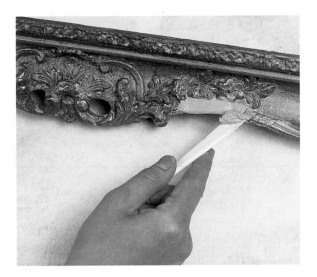

2 Apply more putty into the area to be filled, pressing it firmly with the modeling tool to guarantee a good contact between putty and frame. Scrape away any excess putty as you go along the frame.

3 Using the pointed end of the modeling tool, "draw in" the molded details, matching these markings with those on each side. Keep working this way until the desired effect is achieved and the new patch is sympathetic to the old plasterwork molding.

SEWING TECHNIQUES

If you are handy with a sewing machine, you have the advantage where soft furnishings are concerned. It is useful to be able to replace old pillows or make new covers for chair seats, as these can transform an otherwise respectable armchair. This section covers two simple sewing techniques that give a stylish finishing touch to your home furnishings.

COVERING PIPING CORD

You can buy ready-made welt strips, but finding a match for your chosen fabric can be difficult. Covering the piping cord yourself will solve the problem. Piping cord can be bought in varying thicknesses; I use size 5 or 6 for most upholstery projects. To calculate the amount needed, measure the seams and edges to be piped and add 2 inches (5cm).

1 To make the welt, cut several long strips from your chosen fabric, each about 2 inches (5cm) wide. The strips should be cut on the bias, across the grain of the fabric. Join the strips of fabric together until you have one strip that is long enough for your needs.

2 Fold the fabric strip around the cord and pin the edges together along the length of the cord. Baste as close to the cord as possible, then remove the pins. Place the fabric-covered cord under the zipper foot of the machine and stitch close to the cord using a straight stitch. Trim away the excess fabric evenly so it measures ½ inch (12mm) from the stitching line, then remove the basting thread.

CHOOSING FABRIC

When choosing fabric for most upholstery pieces, make sure it is sturdy and machine washable. For larger pieces, such as the seat base for the day bed, I would recommend washing the fabric before sewing, to preshrink the fibers. When mixing fabrics, always select those that have compatible washing recommendations and are made from the same type of fiber.

MAKING BUTTONHOLES

Buttons add a stylish final flourish to a pillow cover, and for these you will need to make buttonholes. Each one consists of two parallel rows of zigzag stitches and two ends finished with a bar tack. They can be stitched by hand or more quickly with a sewing machine. Consult your machine manual for specific instructions.

The length of the buttonhole opening should equal the diameter of the button plus its height. Test this by making a slit in a scrap piece of fabric to what you think is the right length, and then inserting the button.

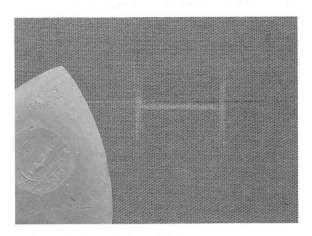

1 Using tailor's chalk, mark the position of the buttonhole on the right side of the fabric.

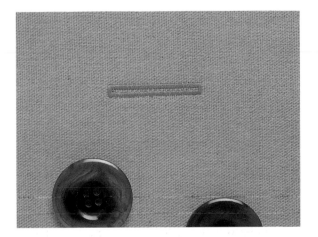

2 Stitch the buttonhole using matching or coordinated sewing thread. The stitched buttonhole should be ⅛ inch (3mm) longer than the marked buttonhole to allow for the stitches at each end.

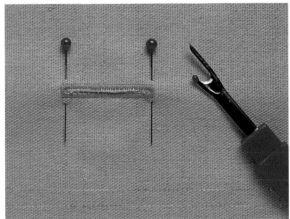

3 To make the opening, place pins at each end of the stitched buttonhole to prevent cutting through the end stitches. Using a seam ripper, carefully slit the fabric down the center of the buttonhole stitches.

There is a huge selection of colorful patterned fabric available. Be bold and go for contrasting stripes, bright checks, or rich floral designs.

THE LIVING ROOM

The living room is usually the one place in the home where there is always room for a spare piece of occasional furniture, the sort that is easily found in most junk outlets. This chapter contains ideas for transforming coffee tables, chairs, a cabinet, and even a day bed using simple paint effects, decoupage, mosaic, and quick and easy sewing techniques.

COUNTRY-STYLE ARMCHAIR

I was fortunate enough to have been given a pair of these wonderful old chairs. If you look past the tired old covers and layers of brown wax, the chair shapes are strong and attractive, perfect for a complete overhaul using paint and fabric. I had stood at the bottom of a ladder as the chairs were precariously handed down to me through an attic hatch, and by the time the second one had arrived, their fate had already been plotted.

The chairs are wonderfully solid and quite heavy, and the only hint of decoration they had were the prettily shaped wooden slats that make up the back rest and a small amount of turned detailing underneath the arm rests. The upholstered pillows were still springy and seemed to have enough life in them, but an inspection hole cut through the upholstery fabric revealed a rather different story. The foam was breaking away at the sides and had a rather crusty-looking appearance on the outside, while things looked very dark and dusty inside. All things considered, I decided it was best to replace the filling with a modern high-density foam block which can be cut accurately to size (using a paper template). Modern foam fillings also have the advantage of having undergone various safety checks required by law, and this assured safety is well worth the additional expense. Check your local newspaper or a business directory for details of foam suppliers or upholsterers who will cut pieces of foam. For larger seat pillows, it is best to choose a dense foam that offers more support.

As the chair has a very solid appearance with only a small amount of decorative detailing (left), color distressing is an ideal treatment which, coupled with the choice of pillow fabric, creates an informal country style (right).

TREATMENT

Once the layers of wax and polish were stripped away (see pages 16–17), the chair was given a coat of white latex primer and was then ready for painting. Since the chair had a solid appearance with only a small amount of decorative detailing, color distressing seemed an ideal treatment and would give a country-style finish. I decided that a bold color would "lift" the chair and settled on a medium blue, revealing shades of pale green underneath.

For some time, the choice of fabric for the covers was not obvious; several remnants of fabric were pinned over the old covers for approval, but none seemed quite right. However, an eclectic mix of several different fabrics combined together, and united only by color and washing compatibility, seemed to work well, and this was the look that was finally settled on. Contrasting cording added a neat finishing touch around the edges of the boxed cover.

MATERIALS

FOR PAINTING:
• Armchair with pillow seat
• Latex primer
• Soft green latex paint
• Medium-blue latex paint
• Wax candle
• Clear furniture wax

FOR THE PILLOWS:
• Brown paper
• Fabric
• Piping cord
• Sewing thread
• Dense foam block
• Buttons

EQUIPMENT

FOR PAINTING:
• Household paintbrush, ½ inch (12mm) wide
• Medium-grit sandpaper
• Medium-gauge steel wool

FOR THE PILLOW:
• Pencil
• Scissors
• Dressmaker's pins
• Tape measure
• Sewing machine

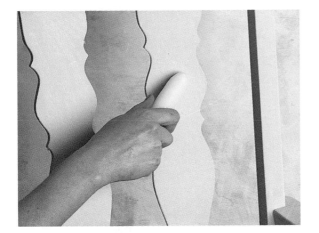

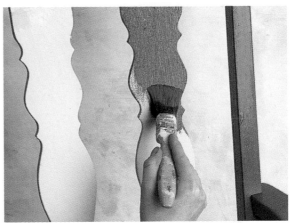

1 Apply two coats of soft green latex paint over the primer, leaving the first coat to dry before applying the second. When the second coat is dry, rub a candle firmly over the paint, particularly on those areas that would show more wear and tear, such as around the turned details. Wherever the candle is rubbed, the top coat will not stick to the underlying base color and will be easily rubbed away.

2 Using a medium blue color, paint the entire surface of the chair, covering the wax completely. Turn the chair upside down to get to the tricky crossbars that are so easy to miss when painting chairs. Brush the paint into the corners and the moldings, using a smaller brush if necessary, and let the paint dry completely.

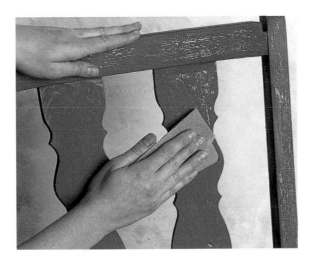

3 Start to rub away at the top coat of paint with a piece of medium-grit sandpaper, following the natural grain of the wood. You should begin to see the underlying color showing through. Continue to rub the color away lightly, concentrating on the arm rests and the back supports. Use light pressure and wear away the paint progressively rather than applying stronger pressure for a shorter time.

4 Using a pad of fine-gauge steel wool, rub clear, soft furniture wax into the sanded surface to protect the paint from further wear and tear and give it a wonderfully smooth finish. The wax and steel wool will remove more of the darker top coat, so do not be surprised to see traces of paint on the steel wool. Keep turning the pad over, and replace it once it has become too clogged up.

MAKING THE CUSHION AND PILLOWS

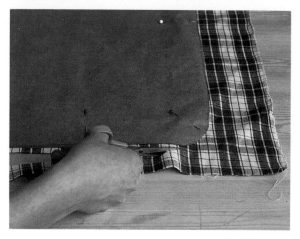

1 If the old cushion fits the space well, place it on a piece of paper. (If it does not, you should use the chair frame as your template instead.) Draw around the outline with a pencil, following the seam line as closely as possible. Cut out the shape from the paper. Check that the pattern is symmetrical by folding it in half.

2 Pin the pattern to the fabric and cut out two pieces, adding an extra ½ inch (12mm) all around for a seam allowance. Measure the depth of the original seat pillow and the length around the four sides. Add ¾ inch (2cm) to each measurement. Using these measurements, cut out a strip of fabric to make a box casing for the cushion.

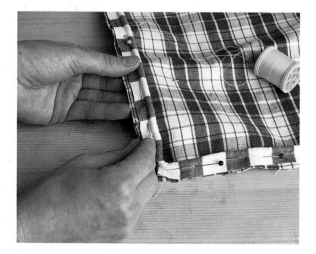

3 Pin the homemade welt (see page 26) around the inside of the top and bottom pieces, aligning the raw edge of the welt with the raw edge of the fabric pieces. Snip almost up to the line of stitches to ease the welt around the corners. To join the ends of the welt, open up the fabric casing and unravel 1 inch (2.5cm) of cord. Trim the strands at slightly different lengths. Twist the strands together, then fold the fabric strip over, and sew to close.

4 Pin and baste the box casing onto the top and bottom pieces using the seam allowance and making sure that the shaped pieces are correctly aligned at both top and bottom. Sew together, leaving a large opening. Turn the pillow cover right side out through the opening and insert a foam block cut to size following the paper pattern drawn in step 1. Slipstitch the opening closed.

5 To make the large buttoned pillow for the backrest of the chair, follow step 1, page 34. First cut out the required fabric piece for the pillow back. Then cut out two fabric pieces for the pillow front measuring the same length as the back; one piece should be the same width and the other piece should be one-quarter of the width of the back piece.

6 Turn under the raw edges. Stitch button-holes (see page 27) down one long side of the small front piece. Pin and baste welt around the edges of the right side of the pillow back. Lay the two front pieces over the back piece, all right sides together and buttonholes and welt to the inside (raw edges out), then pin and stitch around the sides. Turn the cover through to the right side. Sew buttons onto the larger pillow front piece using strong thread. Insert the pillow form and fasten the buttons.

7 To make the throw pillow sham, cut out two cover pieces and, with right sides together, stitch them together around three sides. Then turn under the two raw edges, stitching two fabric ties onto each side. Turn the cover right side out and insert the pillow form. Tie the fabric ties to close. For extra decoration, you can first cover the pillow form in a contrasting fabric. Make this in the same way as above, but stitch up the opening rather than adding ties.

DEED TABLE

A simple, unfussy table such as this one can all too easily be overlooked. My local junk dealer had had this table in his store for weeks, and as soon as I saw it, I snapped it up. The table was cheap, as was to be expected in a secondhand store, but not only had I got a robust, solid wooden table, but the price also included the heavy protective glass top into the bargain. The yellow linen covering the table top was quickly discarded to reveal a wonderfully smooth surface; the linen had actually protected the surface beneath. The glass, although slightly scratched, could easily be cleaned up and then returned to the finished table to protect the surface as before.

I decided to decorate the table with photocopies of old deeds. This treatment is suitable for furniture with simple lines. The original source material that I had for the photocopies consisted of a number of old checks and bills that I had purchased very inexpensively in an antique store. Other calligraphy source material could be taken from copies of old engravings, botanical illustrations, or natural history plates from old books. It can be worth scouring collectors' stands at local flea markets or fairs for examples. Then simply make as many photocopies from the original source as you think you may need. I gave the deeds a slightly antiqued look using cold, strong tea; coffee will have the same effect. Let the liquid "pool" in some areas and remain thin in others to give a more interesting effect.

A glass top is necessary for this paper-lined table. If you aren't lucky enough to have a piece of glass on the table already, you will need to have one cut. Ask the supplier to bevel the edges of the glass to smooth them and so prevent accidents.

TREATMENT

Since the wood was in good condition, all that was required for the preparation was a good sanding, first with medium-grit, and then with fine-grit sandpaper. I decided to decorate the table with photocopies of old deeds and checks, the handwriting on which can often look quite beautiful. The originals are not hard to find and are relatively inexpensive. Dealers that specialize in old postcards, stamps, maps, and bubblegum cards often uncover fine examples of old checks or postcards with decorative handwritten details. Photocopy the handwriting and use the copies, not the originals, to work with. For an antiqued effect, you can age the photocopies using tea or coffee; simply brush a cold, strong solution of either one all over the surface of the photocopies until the desired depth of color is reached.

MATERIALS
- Table
- Brilliant white acrylic primer
- White latex paint
- Photocopied deeds
- Craft glue
- Water
- 4 tea bags
- Gold transfer leaf
- Acrylic gold size
- Photocopied architectural motifs
- Acrylic varnish

EQUIPMENT
- Household paintbrush, ½ inch (12mm) wide
- Pencil
- Sharp scissors

1 Paint the entire surface of the table with a coat of brilliant white acrylic primer; when dry, apply a coat of white latex. Leave to dry. Starting with the table legs, begin to cover the table with the photocopied deeds. First wrap a photocopy around one leg and make a pencil mark on the back of the paper where the two sides meet. Cut the paper to fit the leg. Try to make sure that the edges of the paper do not overlap or wrinkle when glued in position.

2 Dilute craft glue with an equal quantity of water and brush a thin layer onto the table leg. Lay the photocopy over this, aligning the paper with the leg. Gently smooth out any wrinkles with your fingertips, being careful not to tear the paper. Decorate each table leg and the crossbar in the same way.

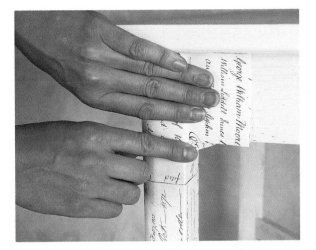

3 After the legs and crossbars have been covered, move on to the sides of the table. When gluing down the paper, wrap the ends of it underneath the table to keep the corners neat. Make sure the lines of script are level, so that it reads either horizontally or vertically.

4 Cover the table top in the same way, overlapping the paper underneath the sides. Overlap it at the corners as well: make a straight scissor cut, then glue the two flaps of paper neatly one on top of the other. Trim and discard any extra bits of paper and press down firmly.

5 Let the glue dry, then tint the paper with a solution of tea. Place four tea bags in a cup of hot water and let this stand until it cools. Brush the cold tea patchily all over the table. Cut out squares of gold transfer leaf and arrange them on the table top. Brush water-based gold size over the areas to be gilded, as shown. When it becomes tacky to the touch, lay the gold transfer leaf squares on the size, shiny side down, burnish, and gently peel off the backing paper. Distress the edges of each piece of gold by scratching them with your fingernail.

6 Cut out the architectural motifs and stick one in the center of each piece of gold transfer leaf using craft glue. Press the edges down firmly and leave to dry. Apply two layers of acrylic varnish over the entire table to seal and protect it. If your table came with a piece of glass, place it on the top, or have a new sheet of glass cut to fit.

STENCILED CABINET

At first glance it would have been easy to disregard this cabinet, since its ugly handles did nothing to echo its simple proportions. However, handles are easy to remove, and this cabinet immediately benefited from such action.

An attractive feature was the small pull-out shelf situated directly beneath its top. The green linoleum covering this extension was in perfect condition, and I knew could be made even glossier with a little linseed oil rubbed into the surface. A pull-out shelf like this is perfect for putting cups or glasses on, thereby reducing the risk of damage to the top painted surface; once the cups or glasses are removed, the shelf is easily pushed back inside the cabinet.

Overall, the unit was in good condition, with no damage to the solid wood on either the outside or the inside. My preparation work would therefore be minimal, which is an obvious advantage when working with junk furniture. Once the handles were removed from the doors, I discovered that both doors could be opened using the narrow beaded edge running vertically along the center. Bearing this in mind, I decided not to replace the handles on the lower

part of the unit since I felt that a simple approach was better. In fact, once all the ghastly handles were removed, I realized that only one small drawer knob was needed, to pull out the shelf. I installed a lock on the drawer, which meant that it could only be pulled out using the key.

A simple unit like this one is equally at home in a living room or bedroom. With its small pull-out shelf, this stenciled cabinet can be used as an occasional bar or as a writing surface.

TREATMENT

I decided to decorate the cabinet using a simple, uncomplicated stencil; this stenciled design would decorate the front and sides of the unit, applied over a washed terra-cotta paint effect. The washed effect would be enhanced by applying the terra-cotta glaze over a medium yellow base coat; this yellow would be faintly visible through the more transparent color, giving a soft dappled effect. This same effect can be achieved using almost any color, provided there is a marked contrast between the base color and the glaze. A deep golden yellow glaze over a pale cream base, for example, would be equally successful.

There was no need for handles as the doors could be opened easily using a raised section along the door opening. The drawer was originally opened with a key, so a new brass lock was installed here. The only replacement hardware that was needed was for the tiny pull-out shelf, which needed a small wooden knob; I painted it to match the base color of the cabinet.

MATERIALS
- Cabinet
- Pale yellow latex paint
- Latex glaze (see page 12)
- Terra-cotta latex paint
- Decorative image (see page 139)
- Sheet of mylar acetate
- Yellow ocher latex paint
- White latex paint
- Black latex paint
- Acrylic varnish

EQUIPMENT
- Paintbrush, ½ inch (12mm) wide
- Glass jar
- Photocopier
- Cutting mat
- Masking tape
- Craft knife
- Saucer
- Stencil brush
- Spray mount

1 Paint the prepared cabinet with a coat of pale yellow latex paint. When dry, mix equal quantities of latex glaze and terra-cotta latex paint together in an old jar, then scrub this over the top of the base color with a household paintbrush. The brush marks should be soft, and the base color should still show through, making a soft, dappled effect.

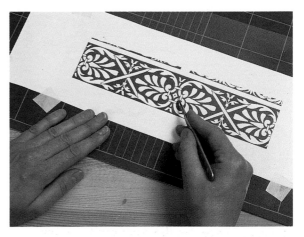

2 Photocopy the decorative image and enlarge it to fit the cabinet. Lay the photocopy down on a cutting mat, place a sheet of mylar acetate on top, and secure the layers with strips of masking tape. Cut the design out of the acetate using a sharp craft knife. Keep the edges and the corners as neat as possible, as this will make the stencil clearer.

3 Place the mylar acetate stencil on the top drawer of the cabinet, making sure that the center of the stencil is directly in line with the center of the drawer. Secure the acetate with masking tape to prevent it from moving.

4 Prepare a saucer with three colors of latex paint: yellow ocher, white, and black. Using a stencil brush, stipple the paint through the stencil, laying the three colors over the top of each other to achieve a mottled effect. The finished result should be subtle and delicately blended.

5 Carefully remove the masking tape and peel back the stencil to expose the stenciled image. Let the paint dry for a few moments before repositioning the stencil.

6 Reposition the stencil over the cabinet; it should fold around corners easily if you apply a light coat of spray mount on the reverse. Apply the stencil paint in the same way as before, using the same three colors. Leave to dry. Using a clean, dry household paintbrush, paint a layer of acrylic varnish over the whole cabinet. Be careful not to brush on so much varnish that it clogs up the spaces between frame, doors, and drawers. Leave to dry. Replace the cabinet handle(s) to complete.

MOSAIC TABLE

One of the most appalling surfaces to decorate is formica, so you would be forgiven for avoiding this coffee table like the plague. Under normal circumstances, I would have avoided it, too; however, I was looking for a suitable surface to use for a mosaic project, and this piece fitted the bill perfectly. Tables are ideal to decorate with mosaic as they can be treated as a flat area, like a blank canvas, and the mosaic built into a picture.

Structurally there was nothing wrong with this table; its legs were secure and there were no chips, cracks, or splits in the formica. It also cost very little, making it an excellent junk find. Although the dark brown color of the base – the result of a nasty brown stain – was not very attractive, once sanded and primed it would be fine for painting.

As formica can be extremely slippery to work with, you may find that building up the sides of the table with the mosaic tiles is a little tricky. The best way to solve this is to work on one side at a time, leaving the glue to set before turning the table over and working on the next side, until all four sides are completed. This process might seem to be somewhat tedious and time-consuming, but it is worth the time that it takes.

Mosaic takes time, rather like working a difficult jigsaw puzzle, but as you see the picture starting to take shape, you'll discover that you can't wait for the image to be completed.

TREATMENT

Before you can begin to decorate the table, you need to find out where you can buy mosaic sheets or tiles. Mosaic sheets can be purchased from some tile suppliers and from specialist mosaic suppliers. Mosaic tiles are also sold through swimming pool suppliers. Check your local telephone directory for details. Usually you will purchase tiles on paper-backed sheets; you need to soak the tiles off the sheets before using them, but this is not a problem as the adhesive is a water-based gum. Occasionally, your supplier may offer a mixed assortment of tiles sold by weight. These are often sub-standard tiles, but they are perfectly good for this type of mosaic project. It may be that the color is a different shade than expected or the ridges on the back of the tile are uneven; in either case, this will not be detrimental to the mosaic, and the cheaper price far outweighs any flaws. Check with your supplier first since these mixed bags are often not on display. Remember, however, that you will not be able to choose any particular colors: you can only take what is offered, then supplement it with the more expensive sheets of mosaic.

Any surface, particularly ultra-smooth formica, must be keyed before the mosaic tiles can be stuck down. This simply means that the tiles need a ridged surface onto which they can stick because they may slide off a smooth surface. The sharp teeth on the edge of a saw are perfect for scratching a toothed surface over formica, composite board, or wood (see page 19). Once the surface is prepared in this way, the mosaic tiles are laid and glued down on top of it, rather like building a jigsaw puzzle.

MATERIALS

- Table
- Glass and ceramic mosaic tiles
- Craft glue
- Tile grout
- Water

EQUIPMENT

- Photocopier
- Pencil
- Paper
- Masking tape
- Carbon paper
- Handsaw
- Tile nippers
- Safety goggles
- Paint bucket
- Putty knife
- Rubber-bladed squeegee
- Cloth

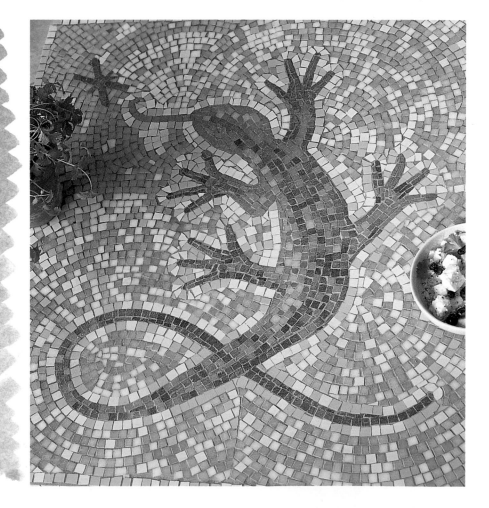

1 Use a photocopier to enlarge the lizard out-line (see page 139) to fit your table. Alternatively, sketch your own simple design for the mosaic. Join several sheets of paper together with masking tape. Sketch your outline on the paper, then transfer the outline to the table top using carbon paper.

2 Scratch the surface and sides of the table with a handsaw to key it (see page 19). Select the colored tiles you wish to use for the design, and lay them over the lizard outline to get an idea of how you would like to arrange the various colors.

3 Wearing safety goggles for protection, snip the tiles into quarters using a pair of tile nippers. Hold the tile with your thumb and index finger and place the cutting edge of the nippers at the edge of the tile. Press the nippers together to break the tile in half, then repeat on each half to make quarters. Squeeze a line of craft glue on the surface of the table and lay the tiles down the spine of the lizard.

4 Build up the mosaic tiles as if you were filling in a jigsaw puzzle. Cut the small quarters to fit tiny gaps, keeping to the outline as closely as possible. As you work around the feet, shape the tiles to fit using the nippers; in broader areas such as the body, glue quarter tiles in place as they are. Butt the edges of the tiles as closely as possible to each other.

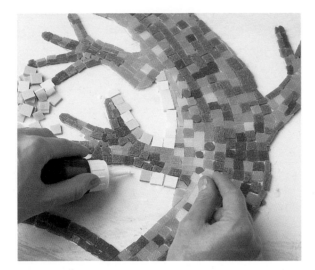

5 Glue the background tiles around the body shape of the lizard, following the contours as closely as possible. This process is a traditional technique called *opus vermiculatum*, meaning literally to "worm around the shape." Use ceramic tiles here to contrast with the glass tiles used for the lizard and accentuate the design.

6 Glue lines of whole, unbroken tiles onto the sides of the table (making sure that the surface is keyed). You may need to tilt the table to prevent the tiles from sliding off. Glue quarter tiles over the edge of the whole tiles along all the side edges. Ceramic tiles are used here to define the edge clearly.

7 Construct the tiny dragonfly before filling in the background. Snip small tile quarters to shape the rounded wings and body. Glue in position. You do not need to add the *opus vermiculatum* around the outline as the insect is not as prominent as the lizard. By avoiding this technique, the eye is automatically drawn to the lizard first, and the dragonfly is secondary.

8 Fill in the rest of the background of the mosaic. Draw semi-circular lines around the lizard as guidelines to follow when laying down the tiles. These lines only roughly follow the lizard's body outline.

9 Following the drawn contours, apply the glue and then the tiles, as before. Use a combination of ceramic and glass tiles to create a varied background effect. These colors were closely matched to create a sandy effect, while the variety of tiles adds a certain sense of vitality to the background.

10 Snip tiny, shaped pieces with the tile nippers to fill any gaps between larger pieces; keep nibbling away at a tile until it fits the gap as tightly as possible. There is an enormous sense of satisfaction when you fill in the last gap, so do persevere.

11 Leave the mosaic to dry overnight. Place the dry tile grout in an old paint bucket, make a well in the center, slowly add cold water, and mix to a soft dropping consistency. Spread the grout over the mosaic with a putty knife. Then, spread it more thinly using a rubber-bladed squeegee. Press down to make sure that all the gaps between the tiles are filled, then scrape away the excess grout.

12 Wipe the surface of the mosaic with a damp cloth to remove the excess grout. Turn the cloth over as the grout builds up on it, and rinse in cold water as and when necessary. Repeat this process on the sides of the table. Leave the mosaic to dry for about 24 hours, occasionally wiping the surface with a damp cloth to remove traces of the grout.

IRONWORK DAY BED

This wrought-iron bed was discovered in an architectural salvage yard and proved to be quite a bargain. There are many fine examples of this type of curly wrought-iron bed, although some can command rather high prices; generally, the more ornate the ironwork, the more expensive the bed.

Two wooden slats were secured with mounting blocks to prevent the slats from moving. The base pillow was cut from a block of high-density foam. If you take the dimensions of the base of the day bed to a specialty foam-rubber dealer or upholsterer, you can get a piece of foam cut specifically to your requirements. The block should be about 5 inches (12.5cm) deep. Choose high-density foam for the seat as this will provide a firmer base. (Lightweight foam will compact easily and will not therefore provide adequate support.)

Two bolster pillows provide the head and foot support of the day bed, while inexpensive throw pillows are propped against the metal back for comfort. The pillows are made from a contrasting tapestry fabric which works well with the fabric used to make the base pillow and the bolsters; too much of any one fabric can overpower the effect, while using a variety adds more pattern. To cover the base cushion, see page 34 for instructions.

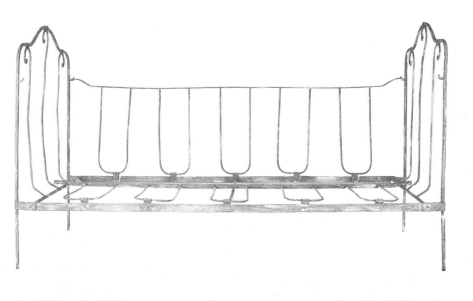

The tapestry fabric of the base cushion works well with the bronze painted frame. Buy some throw pillows in a contrasting fabric or a selection of different coordinated fabrics to prevent the whole look from becoming too stifled.

TREATMENT

The bed frame was relatively easy to prepare for painting. Small patches of rust had started to show through the old paint, so these needed a brisk rub-down with a stiff steel brush. The rest of the painted metal was also rubbed down to make it ready to accept the paint. Red metal oxide primer provides a good base for a top coat of paint and prevents rust from forming again. The most time-consuming aspect of working on a bed frame like this is the painting: all the curly metalwork requires a thorough coat of red oxide. I painted the underside of the bed by turning the frame on its side. Metallic paint was applied once the primer was dry. I chose a bronze metallic paint, but there is a wide choice of metallic colors you can use. To cover the bolster and base pillows (the latter was cut from a block of high-density foam – see page 30) I used a rich tapestry-effect fabric, and the bolster pillows were neatly finished with covered welt and buttons.

MATERIALS

FOR THE FRAME:
- Ironwork crib
- Red oxide metal primer
- Bronze metal paint
- Wood for slats
- Wood for blocks
- Wood glue
- Screws

FOR THE PILLOWS:
- 2 bolster pillow forms
- Fabric
- Contrasting fabric for piping cord
- Sewing thread
- 4 self-cover buttons
- Shaped foam base

EQUIPMENT

FOR THE FRAME:
- Household brush, ½ inch (12mm) wide
- Mineral spirits
- Saw
- Sandpaper
- Pencil
- Screwdriver
- Drill

FOR THE PILLOWS:
- Tape measure
- Scissors
- Dressmaker's pins
- Sewing machine
- Needle

DECORATING THE BED

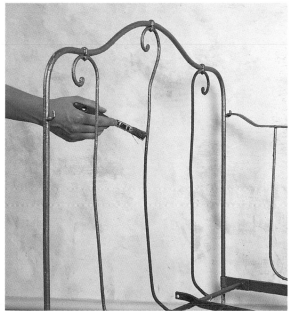

1 Apply a coat of red oxide primer over the entire frame. Do not overload your brush with paint; this will form drips and spoil the paintwork. Turn the frame on its side to reach the underside of the bed to make sure every bit is painted. Leave to dry. Clean the brush using mineral spirits and then apply a coat of bronze metal paint all over the frame.

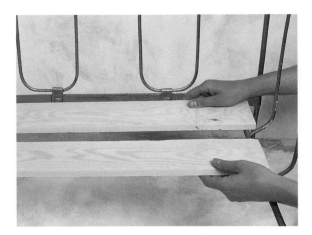

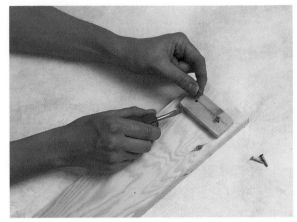

2 Saw two pieces of wood to fit the base of the frame, allowing an overlap of 1 inch (2.5cm) at each end. Sand the cut edges smooth with sandpaper as these will be quite ragged after sawing. Lay the wooden slats over the base to check the fit.

3 Saw four small blocks of wood, slightly narrower than the width of the slats. Lay the slats over the base and mark the point where the blocks are to be mounted. Apply glue on one block, then stick this onto the slat at the marked position. Screw the block in place. Repeat to attach the remaining three blocks.

MAKING THE PILLOW COVERS

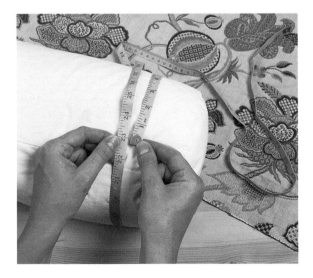

1 To make covers for the bolsters, measure the circumference and add 2 inches (5cm) for a seam allowance. Then measure the radius and add 2 inches (5cm) to this for ends. For each bolster, cut out two rectangles of fabric using these measurements. Next, measure the length of the bolster and add seams; then measure the width (circumference) and add seams. Cut out one piece of fabric for each bolster using these measurements.

2 Make the welt for the edges of the bolsters in a contrasting fabric (see page 26). Pin one of the small rectangles to the short end of the large rectangle, with right sides together and catching the welt inside the two pieces as you go. Stitch using a zipper foot on the sewing machine. Repeat to attach the second small rectangle on the other end of the bolster cover.

3 For each bolster cover, pin together the long edges of the bolster, making sure that the piping is aligned. Stitch down this long edge, and you will now have a large cylinder shape. Turn the cover right side out and put the bolster form inside the cover.

4 Stand the bolster on its end and gather the fabric together in small pleats, joining them together in the center. Push a pin in each pleat to hold it in place and overlap them neatly. Hand-sew the pleats in place. Repeat on the other end of the bolster cover, and on the two ends of the other bolster cover.

5 Cover four buttons with the bolster fabric by wrapping the fabric over the button and securing with a few stitches on the underside, and hand-sew them to the ends of the bolsters.

Decorate your finished pillows with tassels in rich tapestry colors of burgundy and gold to create a sumptuous look.

THE DINING ROOM

Dining rooms may tend toward the spartan
approach in decor, containing a table, chairs,
and a sideboard, and not much else.
However, this chapter demonstrates how you
can transform your dining room into the most
stylish room in the house, by embellishing
several dining-room accessories, and
modernizing a traditional sideboard.

MOCK SANDSTONE TABLE

This unusual wood table had some carved details that unfortunately could not be seen properly because of the overpowering black wood stain. Unfortunately, it would have been impossible to remove the wood stain completely to get back to the natural wood, because dark stains tend to saturate the porous surface of the wood too deeply. However, I felt the table could be painted successfully after a good sanding, and I purchased it with a paint effect in mind. Once the layers of stripper had removed most of the heavy build-up of wax, stain, and varnish from the table, I could start the decorative effect. The table had been heavily stained, which meant that even after stripping, it was still very black. In order to get a good base for the light-colored sandstone paint effect I had decided on, I applied two coats of primer to obliterate the dark color.

When simulating a sandstone effect like this, you may find it useful to look at a real piece of stone while you are working. Look at the composition of the stone and observe how the colors work together, and decide which color is predominant. I used colors that are very close in tone to achieve a soft finish. If you prefer, you could easily substitute a stronger color at any stage of the technique.

The subtle spattered sandstone effect on this occasional table highlights the carved detailing around the edges of both the top and the leg.

TREATMENT

A delicate stone-effect paint finish seemed appropriate for this small table; the carved details on the edge of the table top and on the central support would be subtly high-lighted by the technique.

The speckled stone effect is really only a sophisticated version of the spatter paintings children love to do; the difference is that in this instance the dots are spattered in a con-trolled manner. The delicate spray of dots was created using an old toothbrush: the brush was first dipped into the thinned paint and then a finger was drawn across the stiff bristles to release the paint in a shower of tiny dots. The dots were gradually built up over a dappled paint surface until the speckly appearance of natural sandstone was reached. The amount of spatter can only be judged by eye; you need enough dots to obscure any marks left by the brush, but you also need to see enough of the underlying color to give depth to the paint effect.

MATERIALS
- Table
- Yellow ocher latex paint
- White latex paint
- Dark ocher latex paint
- Moss green latex paint
- Water
- Acrylic varnish

EQUIPMENT
- Household paintbrush, ½ inch (12mm) wide
- Bowl
- Toothbrush
- Nailbrush

1 Paint the table with a coat of yellow ocher latex, then leave to dry. Over this, roughly scumble a layer of white latex paint. This involves half pushing and half dragging the paint onto the surface in a loosely circular movement. You can use the flat part of the brush as well as the tip, and let the color underneath show through the brush marks.

2 When the white paint has dried, stipple a layer of dark ocher latex over the white. To do this, dip a dry paintbrush into a shallow pot of dark ocher paint so that just the tip of the brush is loaded with color. Using a light, jabbing motion, dab the brush onto the table, moving the brush around in different directions so that the marks become varied.

3 Before the stippled ocher paint has dried, scumble a layer of white latex paint over the top, as in step 1. As the paints merge together, a subtle fusion of colors will result. The overall color will now be somewhere between white and yellow ocher.

4 Dilute moss green latex paint in a small bowl, in the proportion of approximately two parts paint to one part water. Dip a toothbrush in the paint and spatter it over the table top by aiming the brush at the table top and lightly and repeatedly flicking your finger over the bristles. Keep reloading the brush and spattering the surface until the whole table is covered with tiny, soft spots of green.

5 Repeat this spattering process using dark ocher latex paint. Dilute the paint slightly as this makes the spattering easier. The whole paint effect should now be getting very soft and stony, with colors merging and no particular color dominating the whole.

6 Apply slightly larger and denser speckles in white latex, using a nailbrush in place of a toothbrush. Use the handle of the toothbrush to flick the bristles. Keep applying these layers of color to the table, with white always being the final layer, until you achieve the desired sandstone effect. Let it dry, then varnish the table to protect the painted surface.

GILDED LAMPS

These two lamps were undoubtedly the cheapest junk find in the book: complete with plugs and one with a working bulb, they cost less than the price of a cup of coffee. Thank heaven for yard sales! Admittedly, they did look rather shabby, but the ceramic bases were not chipped at all, and I thought they would be perfect for gilding. Unfortunately, the shades were not so good, and I decided it would be better to replace them with inexpensive new ones than to renovate the tacky old fabric ones. I took a gamble on whether the lamps would in fact work or not, but at such a low price I could afford the risk. In fact, both lamps did work; all that was needed for one was a new bulb, so my purchase was well rewarded. These junk lamp bases were quite small, but if your junk discoveries have much larger bases, you might like to add more decoration to them, using the gilding as a background color. Had I found larger globe bases, I would have decorated around the gilded globe with decoupage motifs. Tiny moths and insects cut from an old natural history notepad would be perfect, as it would seem that the light had attracted lots of creepy-crawlies toward it. Other images that would work with equal success are butterflies, flowers, or seashells. If you can find them, Dover motif publications provide a wealth of material perfectly suited for decoupage use. Glue the cutouts over the metal leaf using undiluted craft glue, then, when dry, seal with varnish in the usual way.

These natural paper lamp-shades decorated with a simple pattern of pinpricks look very attractive with the gilded bases. Almost any design can be used to create the punched effect.

TREATMENT

I decided to gild both lamp bases; ceramic and glass are good surfaces to gild as they are so smooth. You do, however, need to apply solvent-based gold size or polyurethane varnish, rather than water-based size, over the ceramic base.

As I have said, I decided to replace the shades on the lamps as these were too scruffy to make good. Replacement shades are inexpensive and can be purchased in department stores and many other outlets. I bought natural paper shades, which look attractive with gold transfer leaf, and I decided to decorate them with a punched pattern, which is easily done with a darning needle. Fabric or plastic-coated shades will not punch successfully. The punched pattern is particularly noticeable when the light is switched on, as the light shines brightly through the pattern of tiny, pinpricked holes to create a delicate effect.

MATERIALS
- 2 ceramic lamps
- Strong detergent
- Red oxide metal primer
- Solvent-based gold size or polyurethane varnish
- Gold transfer leaf
- Acrylic varnish
- Paper
- 2 new lampshades

EQUIPMENT
- Cloths
- Fine-grit wet-and-dry paper
- Household paintbrushes
- Photocopier
- Pencil
- Black marker pen
- Scissors
- Masking tape
- Darning needle

1 Wash the lamp bases with strong detergent to remove grime and grease. Dry, then sand them with fine-grit wet-and-dry paper. Paint a thin layer of red oxide metal primer over the surface of each lamp base. This prepares the surface for the gold size and acts as a warm red background color for the gold leaf. Let the primer dry.

2 Using a clean, dry paintbrush, apply a layer of gold size or polyurethane varnish to the dry surface of the lamp base. Hold the lamp carefully, using the bulb-holder as a handle. Leave the size to dry on the base until it is just tacky to the touch.

3 Place the gold transfer leaf over the tacky surface, then press the backing paper down gently. The transfer metal will immediately stick to the tacky size. Then carefully peel away the backing paper.

4 Gild each base in this way. Gently brush over the gold leaf to smooth it in place and brush away any flaky fragments. Buff the surface with a soft dry cloth, and leave to dry overnight. Paint two layers of varnish over the gold leaf to seal. Once dry, the leaf will not tarnish, and it can be wiped clean as necessary.

5 Photocopy the star pattern (see page 141) to the correct size to fit your shade, or draw your own design. Go over the outlines with a black marker pen to make these stronger. Cut away the surplus paper from around the motif so that it fits inside the lampshade. Secure the motif to the inside of the shade with strips of masking tape; make sure the pattern is vertical and not covering a seam in the shade.

6 Begin punching holes in the shade with a darning needle. Hold the needle firmly and rest your hand gently on the lampshade. The lines of the design will be seen more easily if the shade is replaced on the lamp and the lamp is switched on. Tilt the shade away from the bulb and do not punch the darning needle so hard that it touches the bulb. Continue to punch the pattern around the shade.

TREATMENT

Preparation on the sideboard was exhaustive, but worth it in the end. Initially I used a paint stripper all over it to remove the layers of thick brown varnish that had built up over the years. When using strong chemicals such as paint stripper, work outdoors to reduce the build-up of fumes. Wear thick rubber gloves and eye protection. **Caution:** *Masks do not protect you from the fumes of methylene chloride, the toxic active ingredient in stripper.*

Once the varnish had been stripped away, the surface was badly stained and marked, so I used a wood bleach to even out the wood tones and provide a good surface for the decorative treatment. Once again, this chemical preparation is caustic and dangerous to use unless the proper precautions are observed. Follow the manufacturer's guidelines and, again, be sure to wear protective rubber gloves and a vapor respirator.

I decided on a fairly simple decorative treatment for this piece. First I painted a thinned slate-blue latex over the cabinet, then I covered this with pickling wax for a softer effect. The pickling wax was then buffed to a sheen using a soft cloth.

MATERIALS

- Sideboard
- Varnish stripper
- Vinegar
- Water
- Wood bleach
- Dark blue latex paint
- Pickling wax

EQUIPMENT

- Rubber gloves
- Household paintbrushes, ½ inch (12mm) wide
- Scraper
- Stiff steel brush
- Coarse- and medium-grade steel wool
- Bowl
- Cloths
- Glass jar
- Steel ruler
- Pencil
- Drill
- Screwdriver

1 Lay the sideboard on its back or side in order to work on a flat surface. Wearing rubber gloves for protection, dab generous amounts of varnish stripper over the entire varnished surface, according to the manufacturer's instructions. Leave the stripper to work on the varnish.

2 When the stripper starts to work, you will notice the old layers of varnish starting to bubble and to blister. Leave the stripper on the surface of the cabinet for the manufacturer's recommended time. Start to scrape away the build-up of old varnish layers.

3 Keep scraping the surface of the wood until the surface is clear. Use a soft brass or scrub brush, or a toothbrush to get at carved details and other parts that the scraper will not reach into. Work *away* from yourself to avoid being splattered with a shower of stripper and varnish from the brush.

4 When the sideboard is almost free of stripper, rub the entire surface with a pad of medium-grade steel wool. Work with the grain to clean the surface of the wood and to get rid of the last traces of stripper. Then go over the surface with fine-grade steel wool. Wipe the surface with mineral spirits. Soak a cloth in this solution, then wipe it over the sideboard. Rub the surface well, then leave to dry thoroughly.

5 Apply wood bleach over the surface of the sideboard to even up the tones of the wood. **Caution:** *Wood bleach has two parts, lye and hydrogen peroxide, both of which are very caustic to the skin, so wear long heavy-duty rubber gloves and goggles.* Brush the first part of the bleach onto the cabinet according to the instructions on the package.

6 When this first part is slightly dry, brush on the second part of the bleach. Stipple the solution into the carved details, always taking care not to splash the solution toward you. Wear gloves and protective eye goggles.

7 When this second part of the treatment is quite dry, it can leave a powdery white deposit on the surface of the wood. Wipe the surface clear with a mild vinegar solution; follow the manufacturer's instructions for detailed advice. Let it dry.

8 When the surface of the sideboard is completely dry, it can be decorated. Dilute some dark blue latex paint with cold water in the proportion of two parts paint to one part water, and mix together thoroughly in an old jar. Brush the paint over the whole unit. Although the color looks very dark at this stage, it will be lightened considerably with pickling wax.

9 Let the blue base coat dry completely. Using a soft cloth, rub a generous amount of pickling wax over the whole surface. Rub the wax deep into the carved details and into the recessed areas of the sideboard. Let the porous surface absorb as much wax as possible.

10 Buff the pickle-waxed surface with a clean dry cloth to remove excess wax and create a soft sheen. Turn the cloth over as the excess wax builds up and replace the cloth if necessary. The recessed areas will hold the wax, which will enhance the limewashed effect.

11 If you intend to reposition the handles, mark the new position carefully using a steel ruler and a pencil. You will need to determine new positions for the screws; mark these positions accurately on the face of the sideboard with faint pencil marks.

12 Make new screw holes with a drill. Work directly above the new position and choose the appropriate bit for the drill. The bit should be the same diameter or slightly smaller than the shaft of the screw you will be using for the tightest grip.

13 Attach the handles to the sideboard. On this sideboard, the screws are screwed into the handle from the back of the door. Remove any pencil marks remaining on the wood by polishing with a soft cloth.

VERDIGRIS CHANDELIER

I found this beautiful metal chandelier in the back of a real junk store and coveted it immediately. It was as shabby as the store itself and covered in a mass of cobwebs, but the spiders would just have to find another home.

The chandelier had the potential for electrification, but on closer inspection I found that the cables were badly damaged; however, I could unscrew the fixtures and use the chandelier for candles. If you find a similar chandelier and are interested in electrifying it, it is worth noting that some electrical appliance outlets carry out an electrification service if required.

Although it was shabby, this chandelier was very ornate, and the small leaf scrolls on it seemed perfect for a little gilding decoration. I tend to use less expensive composition metal leaf as opposed to the rather expensive gold equivalent for gilding. When applying the metal leaf, let a little of the red oxide primer show through from underneath to simulate real gesso and bole, which would traditionally have been used under gilding.

The arms of the chandelier and the rest of the frame were ideal for a metal paint finish. Verdigris is traditionally seen on copper or bronze and is the result of years of neglect and weathering. Here, I used a combination of bluish-green paints to simulate the effect. Because the surface is metal, a metal primer is required. Then solvent-based paints or latex ones can be used to create this paint effect.

The bright greenish blue verdigris colors work very well with the antiqued gilding. This battered old chandelier started life as an unwanted, cheap junk store find, but it is completely transformed with this simple paint effect and a little gilding.

TREATMENT

The condition of the chandelier was pretty good underneath all the cobwebs, and there were no old paint layers to strip away. However, the rusty metal needed a thorough rub-down, and the twisting ironwork meant that there were plenty of nooks and crannies where the rust had really taken hold.

Once the surface was clean, the delicate, elegant leaf forms of the chandelier seemed to cry out for a touch of gold. For such projects I use real gold leaf or composition metal, which gives the appearance of real gold leaf at a fraction of the cost. I prefer to use metal leaf rather than gold metallic paints, as it has a superior finish and is more characteristic of real gold. Metallic paints tend to dry to a flat finish which is dull by comparison.

By way of contrast, I thought the solid, classic lines of the iron framework would be suited to the antique look of bluish green verdigris. Verdigris is the brightly colored tinge that occurs naturally when untreated bronze or copper meet the elements, and is often seen on old weathervanes. You may also see it more unwelcomely around the copper plumbing pipes in your own home. Although it takes many years to achieve naturally, with a little patience you can create something similar using paint. First the framework needs to be bronzed. Then the colored paints are built up on top for some instant aging.

MATERIALS

- Metal chandelier
- Red oxide metal primer
- Bronze metal paint
- Turquoise eggshell paint
- Duck's-egg blue eggshell paint
- Fine white plaster of Paris
- Acrylic gold size
- Gold transfer leaf
- Clear polyurethane varnish
- Spray varnish

EQUIPMENT

- Medium-grit sandpaper
- Stiff wire brush
- Household paintbrushes, ½ inch (12mm) and ¼ inch (6mm) wide
- Masking tape
- Mineral spirits
- Clean dry cloths
- Bowl
- Artist's brush

1 Unscrew and take apart the candle-holders and any other parts that you need to get to. Prepare the metal by rubbing it with sandpaper and a stiff wire brush. Then paint the whole chandelier with a coat of red oxide metal primer. When it is dry, mask the areas to be gilded with masking tape.

2 Paint the framework with bronze metal paint, taking care to avoid drips. Use this paint fairly thinly and make sure it is well mixed before starting. Keep turning the chandelier around and upside down to make sure you have painted the entire framework. Leave to dry.

3 Using a small paintbrush, stipple patches of turquoise eggshell paint over the bronze. Apply the paint sparingly using the tip of the brush. About half the area should be stippled at this stage, and the rest should remain bronze. Leave to dry; wash the brush in mineral spirits.

4 Stipple patches of duck's-egg blue eggshell paint over the bronze and the turquoise. Let some of the bronze show through; the result should be an even distribution of the three colors. Remember to paint the underside since the chandelier will be seen from below. Leave the paint until it is almost dry, but still tacky.

5 Press a clean dry cloth into a bowl of dry plaster of Paris, and quickly dab a thin layer of the powder over the tacky surface of the paint. The effect should be quite subtle, giving just the illusion of a layer of dust. Cover the whole frame in this way.

6 Gently peel off the masking tape from the leaves. Using an artist's brush, apply a thin layer of gold size over the metal leaves. You must bear in mind that wherever the size goes, the gold leaf will stick. Leave the size until it is just tacky to the touch.

7 Lay the gold transfer leaf over the tacky size, shiny side down. Press the backing paper down gently with your fingers and the metal will adhere instantly to the size. Carefully peel away the backing paper to reveal the gilded leaf. You may need to give a second application to cover odd cracks where the gold leaf has not stuck; alternatively, you may prefer to leave some of the red oxide peeking through, as it can look very attractive.

8 Using a clean, dry brush, gently flick it over the surface of the gold to loosen any excess bits of gold leaf. At the same time, the brush will press the gold down securely in place. Buff the surface with a soft, dry cloth.

9 Seal and protect the transfer leaf, but not the verdigris framework, with a coat of polyurethane varnish. Leave to dry thoroughly. Screw the fixtures back into place. Lightly spray the verdigris paintwork with a can of matte spray varnish. This will protect the finish and hold the dusty layer in place.

MIRROR FRAME

I was delighted to find this old frame at a yard sale. Some of the ornate plasterwork had been knocked, and bits had dropped off, but it was repairable. A dull metal paint had been applied over the whole frame, which gave the molding a particularly uninteresting look, and I'm sure this was why the frame had not been sold immediately. Secondhand stores and yard sales generally supply a vast selection of frames like this, and it should not be difficult to find your own bargain. Small or large, heavily molded or simply carved, the type of frame should not matter too much since decorating techniques are usually adaptable for most frames.

The silver leaf gilding used on this frame is in fact made from sheets of aluminum rather than silver itself, and this does make it more affordable. Most good art-supply stores should be able to supply this product. The silvered effect gives a contemporary feel to an otherwise traditional mirror. If you prefer a more traditional look, simply replace the silver aluminum leaf with a gold-colored

substitute. Both products are applied in the same way, and both should be sealed afterward to prevent tarnishing.

A glass supplier will cut a mirror to size if you take along the appropriate measurements. Secure the glass in the frame and back it with a piece of plywood, then tack it down securely to hold the mirror in place.

The silver effect has an antiqued look if parts of the background color are allowed to show through the leaf. For a more traditional effect, use red gesso and bole under a gold leaf.

TREATMENT

This ornate frame was perfect for gilding. However, rather than using the more familiar gold-colored metal leaf, I decided to opt for a more contemporary look and chose to use imitation silver leaf. This is in fact made from aluminum rather than silver, and although it is slightly more expensive than gold-colored composition metal, it is still remarkably good value. Most art suppliers will stock metal leaf and water-based gold size.

Rather than striving to achieve a perfect covering with the aluminum leaf, I chose to allow the base to show through in patches. If you prefer, you could apply gold-colored metal leaf instead of silver, but in this case it would look better if the frame was painted deep terra-cotta to simulate traditional red gesso and bole, before gilding.

The gilded frame was varnished with clear acrylic varnish to protect the metal leaf. You could use polyurethane varnish; this has a slightly yellowing effect on metal leaf, and gently softens and ages it.

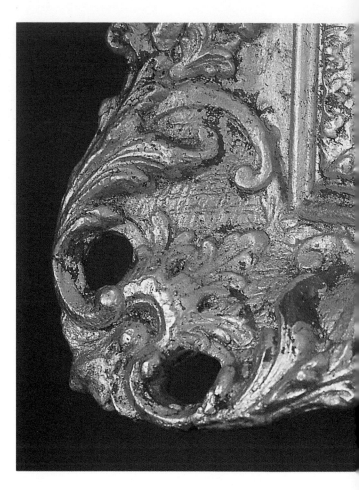

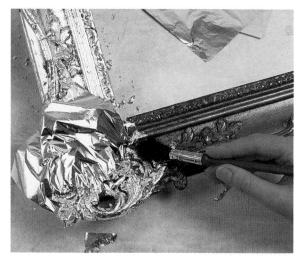

1 Clean the surface of the frame to remove any dusty or flaky patches. Using a small brush, apply a layer of water-based gold size over the frame, working on a small area at a time. Dab the size into the details of the molding, taking care not to get a build-up of size in the hollows. Leave the size to dry until it is slightly tacky.

2 Take one layer of aluminum metal leaf at a time, and lay it over the tacky size, silver side down. The leaf will bond to the sticky size on contact. Gently press the aluminum leaf into the moldings of the frame using a dry brush.

MATERIALS

•Frame
•Acrylic gold
size
•Aluminum
metal leaf
•Acrylic varnish

EQUIPMENT

•Household
paintbrushes,
½ inch (12mm) and
¼ inch (6mm)
wide
•Clean soft cloth

3 Continue applying the aluminum leaf all around the frame. Once the size has dried, the leaf will no longer stick, so work on one small area at a time. If, after you have finished gilding, there are any large areas without aluminum, reapply the size and then the leaf, as before. Buff the surface with a clean soft cloth.

4 Leave the size to dry for about an hour, then apply two layers of acrylic varnish. Move the paintbrush around all the detailed molding, but as with the layer of size, avoid a build-up of excess varnish.

THE KITCHEN

The heart of the home deserves a facelift every now and then. This chapter does that with its cheerful and innovative ideas for revamping tired wooden kitchen chairs, transforming a decrepit hutch, updating a couple of cabinets, and rescuing a tatty old tray. To get started, all you need is paint, paper, and a sheet of aluminum.

PAINTED CHAIRS

Chairs like these can be found in secondhand stores and yard sales across the country. The chair seen here in its dilapidated "before" state was deemed unsaleable at a local auction, and the auctioneer, who thought it was only fit for firewood, was glad to give it to me. Sadly, I think too many old chairs end up this way, although with a little basic mending, they can be quickly restored. If your chair needs repair work, do this first – before stripping or washing down. Leave the repairs to set firmly if any wood glue has been used; several hours should be enough, but it is preferable to leave them overnight.

Most wooden kitchen chairs like these are finished simply with polish or wax and very little else, which makes them perfect for painting. All that is needed is a brisk rub-down using a pad of steel wool dampened with mineral spirits, which will soften and lift off the wax. Turn the chair upside down to access the underside. Once the polish or wax has been stripped away, leave the chair to dry out thoroughly before painting.

Almost any decorative treatment can be carried out on wooden kitchen chairs like these; choose colors to suit your existing furniture. Often a room may suit an eclectic assortment of painted chairs, or you may choose to paint only two chairs out of a set of six; in this case, paint the shabbiest chairs in the set and simply wax those remaining.

Such robust kitchen chairs are perfect for a quick paint transformation. Choose a decorative treatment to suit your room and alter the colors as appropriate to your own home.

BLUE-CHECKED CHAIR

Once the repair work had been finished on the broken chair, the decorative paint treatment could begin. All three chairs required a vigorous rub-down with steel wool and mineral spirits, to clean off the years of dirt and grime that had slowly built up. As a rule, once the first layers of wax are softened and removed, the task becomes much easier, so don't abandon your furniture if this initial layer proves difficult – just grit your teeth and keep going. Keep turning the steel wool over as the grime builds up on the pad, and replace the pad as necessary; wear rubber gloves to protect your hands. You will need to work much harder around the base of the spindles at the back of the chair and around the turned detailing on the legs, because these are the areas that generally harbor most of the dirt and grime. The wood will start to look much cleaner as the mineral spirits dries from the surface.

1 Using a sharp kitchen knife, cut a piece of household cellulose sponge into a square, approximately 1 inch (2.5cm) wide. Work on a cutting mat to protect your work surface. Paint the prepared chair with a layer of white latex primer and let it dry. Then apply two more coats of flat white latex paint.

MATERIALS

- Wooden chair
- White latex primer
- Flat white latex paint
- Blue latex paint
- Furniture wax

EQUIPMENT

- Sharp kitchen knife
- Cellulose decorator's sponge
- Cutting mat
½ inch (12mm) wide
- Tape measure
- Pencil
- Plate
- Eraser
- Fine artist's brush
- Medium-grade steel wool
- Soft cloth

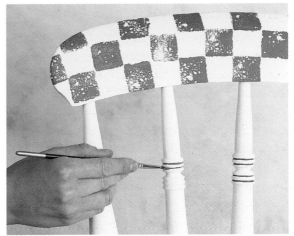

2 When the chair is dry, mark squares on the backrest in pencil. Divide the backrest into three equal horizontal sections using a tape measure and a pencil. Start in the middle of the backrest, where the area is flattest, and draw parallel lines out to each side. Then draw vertical lines at 1-inch (2.5cm) intervals. Repeat to mark the seat. Dip the sponge square into a plate of blue latex paint, and print onto the chair in alternate squares to make a checked pattern.

3 Let the paint dry, then remove any visible pencil lines with an eraser. Dilute a little blue latex paint with water and, using a fine artist's brush, paint delicate lining details around the spindles of the chair back; any turned detailing looks effective decorated in this way. You will need a steady hand to maintain an even line; if necessary, support your painting hand at the wrist with your other hand.

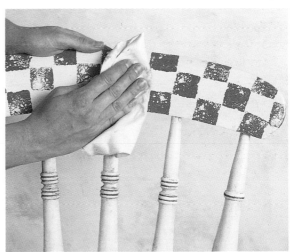

4 Let the paint dry. If the chair is to be used only for display, apply colored furniture wax over the entire surface, using a pad of medium-grade steel wool. Use a circular motion to apply the wax. The wax protects the surface and gives an antiqued finish. (Colored wax tends to rub off.)

5 Using a soft cloth, buff the waxed surface to a soft sheen. Those areas that would naturally see a build-up of darker wax should be rubbed lightly, so as not to remove too much wax. The wax will protect the chair from general knocks, spills, and splashes, but subsequent coats should be applied every six months.

TARTAN PLAID CHAIR

Plaid paint effects have been enjoying a revival over the past few years, and examples can be seen on practically everything from bath towels to bone china. The colors can be tailored to suit your own requirements. Here, lime green and orange are used together for a dramatic effect, but more subtle colors, such as pale blue and slate gray, would work equally well.

Make sure there is a strong contrast between the printed squares which form the background of the plaid, and the delicate hand-painted lines. A steady hand is needed to maintain even painted lines; a drawn pencil line will keep the loaded brush on the right track, but those with wobbly hands may need to tip the chair so that the backrest is lying flat on a table surface, making painting easier. It would be a good idea to have a practice run first.

MATERIALS
- Wooden chair
- Latex primer
- Soft green latex paint
- Lime green latex paint
- Orange acrylic paint
- Acrylic varnish

EQUIPMENT
- Household paintbrushes, ½ inch (12mm) wide
- Tape measure
- Cellulose decorator's sponge
- Sharp kitchen knife
- Pencil
- Plate
- Straight-edged ruler (optional)
- Fine artist's brush

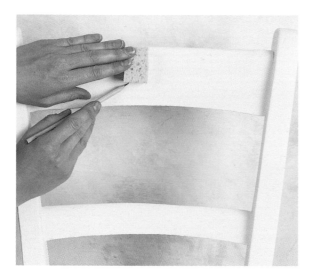

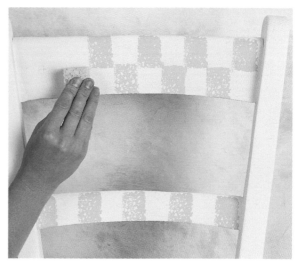

1 Prime the surface as on page 86. Then paint the chair with two coats of soft green latex paint and leave to dry. Measure the back of the chair to determine the size of the printed squares, as outlined in step 2 of the Blue-checked Chair (see page 87). Cut a small piece of sponge according to these measurements, using a sharp kitchen knife. Plot the positions of the squares on the chair using the cut sponge as a guide, and marking with faint pencil marks.

2 Dip the sponge into a plate of lime green latex paint and print the color directly onto the back of the chair using the pencil marks as guides. Do not be tempted to press the sponge down too hard as this may blur the print. The sponge will leave characteristic holes in the paint which adds to the printed character. Keep printing with the sponge to decorate the entire backrest, dipping the sponge in the paint as you need it.

 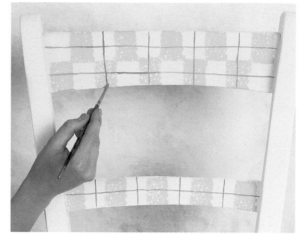

3 Once the paint is dry, lightly mark the vertical and horizontal lines that dissect the checked squares with a pencil. It is quite easy to work by eye, but use a flexible straight-edged ruler if you think you need a guide. Mark both the long horizontals and the shorter verticals.

4 Dilute a little orange acrylic color with some water. Using a fine artist's brush, paint along the pencil lines, holding the brush steady. Let the paint dry. If your chair has turned detailing on the legs, you may wish to add some fine lines here using the same colors. When dry, seal and protect the surface with a coat of acrylic varnish. Leave to dry.

DAMASK STENCILED CHAIR

Stenciling is a quick way to add decoration to a piece of furniture, and the flat seat and backrest of a chair make perfect stenciling surfaces. If you have several chairs to choose from, the ones most suitable for stenciling are those with completely flat backrests and seats; some seats curve inward slightly, whereas others are flatter.

Stencils can be bought in almost every decorating and hardware store, although it is not difficult to make your own stencil for very little expense. You will need transparent mylar acetate, which is easier to cut than the more traditional oiled manila paper; a good art or craft supply store should stock it. A cutting mat is convenient, but is not absolutely essential; ordinary cardboard, a piece of glass, or an old vinyl tile are cheaper alternatives for protecting your work surface. Use a craft knife to cut out the stencil.

MATERIALS
- Stencil motif (see page 140)
- Transparent mylar acetate
- Wooden chair
- Latex primer
- Soft yellow latex paint
- Dark ocher latex paint
- Yellow ocher latex paint
- Polyurethane varnish
- Raw umber artist's oil color (optional)

EQUIPMENT
- Photocopier
- Masking tape
- Cutting mat
- Craft knife
- Household paintbrushes, ½ inch (12mm) wide
- Stencil brush
- Plate

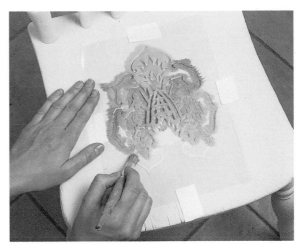

1 Photocopy the stencil motif shown on page 140 (or use your own motif) and enlarge it to the required size. Tape the photocopy onto a cutting mat and tape the transparent mylar acetate on top of this. Starting from the center and working out, cut out the darker areas of the design using a sharp craft knife.

2 Prime the surface as on page 86. Then add two coats of soft yellow latex paint, leaving the first coat to dry before applying the second. When dry, position the stencil over the center of the seat. Anchor the mylar acetate in place with masking tape. Using a stencil brush, stipple dark ocher and yellow ocher latex paint from a plate through the cut stencil, blending the colors. Practice stippling on a piece of scrap first.

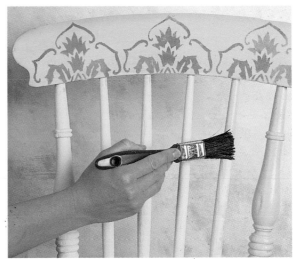

3 Once the first motif is completed, lift up the stencil and reposition it on another part of the seat. Stipple on the paint, blending the two colors together to create an interesting effect. If the seat area is slightly curved, hold the stencil down lightly with your fingertips while stenciling, in order to maintain a good contact with the surface. Stencil the chair backrest in the same way. Let the paint dry.

4 Apply a coat of tough polyurethane varnish all over the chair to protect the painted surface. To enrich the color of the chair, as shown here, tint the varnish with a small amount of raw umber artist's oil color before applying it. Turn the chair upside down to varnish the underside. Let it dry.

KITCHEN HUTCH

The two parts of this hutch were found in separate stores. The base looked very shabby and had suffered several paint treatments; the doors were hanging off, and the top needed some attention. Despite these drawbacks, it seemed a good purchase: the price was low, as expected for a junk find, and there were no visible signs of woodworm or irreparable damage.

The top piece, on the other hand, had been simply treated with one layer of a rather nasty brown varnish that would be easy to remove. The seller seemed anxious to get rid of the top, so I made him an offer and, after a little bargaining, bought it for a good price. Once the two pieces were put together, they suited each other so well that I decided to treat them as one piece of furniture and make a practical hutch. The top was a touch wider than the base, but when hung slightly above it, the difference was barely noticeable.

On the base unit, the hinges were removed and the old holes filled with wood putty. New hinges were then positioned slightly lower down, and new holes were made for the hardware, which made the hinges much more stable.

The top of the base unit needed a few carefully positioned screws to hold it securely to the frame. These were countersunk and then filled. Apart from these minor repairs, nothing else needed fixing.

The finished hutch looks like a handmade piece of furniture rather than the two pieces of unwanted junk that were bought for a pittance.

TREATMENT

Once the two hutch pieces were prepared and ready for painting, I was able to look at the unit as a whole. Colors for furniture will often be dictated by the decor of the room, although they should not necessarily be chosen to blend in; often a unit can look most effective if it is painted to stand out from other furniture. In a pale yellow kitchen, for example, this strong green hutch would look wonderfully dramatic.

The black and white artwork for the design that I used on the door panels had been sitting on my desk for rather a long time, and I was determined to use it in some form or another for decorating a piece of furniture; when I looked at the two paneled doors, it sprang immediately to mind as the proportions seemed right. In fact, the designs were slightly too wide for the door panels, but I used a photocopier to elongate them to fit the proportions as necessary.

MATERIALS
- Unit top and base
- White latex primer
- Terra-cotta latex paint
- Dark green latex paint
- Photocopied motif (see page 140)
- Soft gray acrylic color
- Black acrylic color
- Acrylic varnish
- Cup hooks and screws

EQUIPMENT
- Household paintbrushes, ½ inch (12mm) wide
- Candle
- Medium-gauge steel wool
- Carbon paper
- Masking tape
- Pencil
- Artist's brushes
- Screwdriver

DECORATING THE TOP PIECE

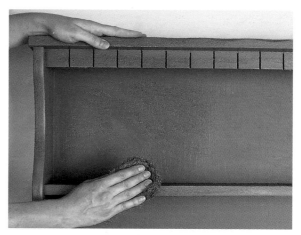

1 After stripping the old varnish from the unit, apply a coat of white latex primer all over, followed by a coat of terra-cotta latex paint. When it is dry, rub the surface with a candle. The wax will resist the next layer of paint, making it easier to rub back. Apply more wax around those areas that would naturally receive most wear and tear, such as the corners and along the front of the shelves.

2 Paint the entire unit with an even coat of dark green latex paint. In areas where the wax candle has been heavily worked, you will find that the paint is difficult to apply. This is where the wax resists the wet paint. Let the paint dry, then fold up some steel wool into a neat pad and rub it over the surface. Those areas which had been rubbed with the wax candle will now begin to show through as red.

DECORATING THE BASE

1 Apply a coat of white latex primer over the prepared base, then when dry, apply two coats of dark green latex paint. This base unit will have a solid color, unlike the top, which has a broken-color effect. When the paint is dry, lay a sheet of carbon paper, right side down, on the panel of one door. Lay a photocopied motif (see page 140) over this, secure it with strips of masking tape, and draw around the outline of the design with a pencil.

2 Repeat this on the second door panel, to produce two identical panels. Use the carbon-paper trace lines as a guide for painting. Fill in the solid parts of the design with soft gray acrylic color using an artist's brush. Some parts of the carbon outline will remain unpainted; these are the shadow areas to be filled in later.

3 Once the soft gray color is dry, tint a little black acrylic color with the gray to make a darker shade of gray; use this to fill in the shadow areas. Use a finer artist's brush to do this, and work your way from the top of the panel down to avoid smudging.

4 When the acrylic colors have dried completely, varnish the whole unit. This will provide a tough, durable protective layer which will help to resist knocks, scrapes, and general wear and tear. It will also provide a washable surface for easier cleaning. Replace the handles on the base unit and screw cup hooks into the top of the hutch to complete the unit.

DECOUPAGED TRAY

You would be forgiven for not picking this tray out of a bargain box no matter how cheap the price. Yet when you see the finished tray decorated with stylish vegetable motifs and rustic paint color, it is difficult to see why there would be any hesitation about buying it. This tray was particularly attractive because of the solid brass handles at the sides; although these were badly tarnished, a quick rub-down with brass polish would soon revitalize them.

If you are looking for a secondhand tray, always check that the handles are secure or can be repaired easily. Another obvious criterion of a good tray, although this can sometimes be overlooked, is that the base should be absolutely flat. Often trays can become warped and buckled, particularly if they are stored in damp conditions. Pick the tray up, examine it, and place it on a flat surface; if there is any hint of a wobble, put it back. The plywood base of this tray was in reasonable condition; there were no splits or cracks which would have

deterred me from buying it. Always check the underside of trays for splits in the wood, as splinters would scratch a table surface.

I used vegetable decoupage motifs to decorate this tray, but you could easily substitute another image if you prefer. Select images that are printed on thick, good-quality paper, as a thinner paper may allow the print on the reverse to show through.

The rustic, wax-distressed paint finish on the sides of this tray complement these quirky vegetable motifs taken from a copyright-free sourcebook.

TREATMENT

Preparing the tray for painting required lots of rubbing with a pad of steel wool and mineral spirits. The old layer of varnish was flaky and easy to remove this way. If there had been several layers of varnish or lacquer, it would have been easier to remove them with a more powerful paint and varnish stripper. The tray then had to be sanded lightly and the cracks and holes filled before the decorative painting could be started.

I decided to use a simple rustic paint finish for the tray. This involved applying a top coat of latex over a base coat. The top layer was then worn away to allow the base color to show in patches. The colors used were characteristically muted: moss green and "dirty" cream were used for the top colors, and yellow ocher was used as the base. Terra-cotta or slate blue would work equally well as base colors.

The vegetable decoupage motifs were taken from a copyright-free sourcebook and enlarged on a photocopier. They were then tinted, which can be done with watercolors, acrylics, colored latex paints, or even colored crayons or pastels. As the print on photocopies can sometimes bleed, it is a good idea to seal the tinted copies with a pastel fixative; hairspray is an excellent substitute for this. From experience, I find it useful to cut out more copies than you think you may need, as it allows you to play around with the various motifs on the tray until you are satisfied with their final arrangement.

MATERIALS
- Tray
- White latex primer
- Yellow ocher latex paint
- Moss green latex paint
- Cream latex paint
- Vegetable motifs
- Watercolor paints
- Pastel fixative or hairspray
- Craft glue
- Water
- Oil-based varnish

EQUIPMENT
- Masking tape
- Household paintbrushes, ½ inch (12mm) wide
- Candle
- Medium-grade steel wool
- Photocopier
- Fine artist's brush
- Small, sharp scissors
- Pencil
- Small sponge

1 Wrap masking tape around the brass handles of the tray to protect them from the paint. Paint a layer of white latex primer over the entire surface of the tray, both underneath and on top. When dry, paint the tray with a coat of yellow ocher latex paint and leave this to dry, too. Rub the top surface and the sides of the tray with a candle. Paint the sides of the tray with a coat of moss green latex paint. Do not worry about perfect coverage with this color since it will be rubbed back later. Some areas of paint will remain damp because the underlying wax prevents the paint from drying; this will be removed later.

2 Apply a coat of cream latex paint over the base of the tray, brushing in one direction. Aim for an even coverage of paint, but don't worry if traces of the underlying color show through; this will add to the finished paint effect. Let the paint dry.

3 Fold under the ends of a piece of medium-grade steel wool to make a neat pad and rub it over the surface of the tray. Rub some areas of the tray more than others, such as around the handles and at the corners, to simulate natural wear and tear.

4 Photocopy a selection of vegetable motifs. Using a fine artist's brush, tint the motifs with diluted watercolor paints, allowing the underlying motif outlines to show through. When dry, seal the motifs with a coat of pastel fixative or hairspray. Carefully cut out the motifs with a pair of small, sharp scissors, following the outlines as closely as possible. Cut more motifs than you think you may need, as these will be useful when you are arranging them. Position the motifs on the tray, rearranging them until you are satisfied with the design. Mark the final position of each motif faintly in pencil.

5 Dilute a little craft glue with a small amount of water and brush this onto the back of each tinted motif in turn. Position the motifs neatly on the surface of the tray using the pencil marks as guides. Press the motifs from the center out with your finger to remove any air bubbles which would spoil the effect of the decoupage. Using a small, damp sponge, wipe any excess glue from the surface of the motifs, gently blotting the area around each motif. Let the decoupage dry overnight. Then protect and seal the surface of the tray with at least two coats of clear oil-based varnish.

STAMPED CABINET

Small cabinets like this one are easy to find in secondhand outlets, so it makes sense to select one that is going to be easy to prepare. Had this unit been thickly painted with a heavy gloss finish, for example, I would probably have given it a cursory glance and then moved on to something else. As it was, the piece had been simply finished with varnish, so the preparation only involved using a commercial varnish stripper.

The cabinet had a certain appeal; its slightly bowfronted doors were unusual and attractive. The lack of moldings meant that a decorative paint treatment would not be hindered by fussy details. The condition of the unit was pretty good; there was no splitting in the veneer surface, and the hinges were strong and secure. Another important detail was that the drawer still glided easily on the runners.

I decided to decorate the cabinet with a stamped motif. Stamping is a recent phenomenon that can produce some wonderful results. In many ways, it is easier than stenciling and can be applied to almost any surface, provided the right paint is used. Making and using your own stamping block is a great boon, particularly as

printing blocks are expensive. This particular stamp is outlined at the back of the book for you to copy, but if you prefer, it is possible to choose another stamp design.

The colorwashed paint finish is applied to the unit before stamping. Almost any color would be successful on a small piece like this; take inspiration from the rest of your kitchen.

TREATMENT

Once the piece had been stripped of its brown varnish, all that was needed was a thorough rub-down with sandpaper before the decoration could begin.

I had decided to stamp the cabinet. Stamped motifs always look better printed over a soft dappled paint finish; here, a creamy-colored scumble glaze was washed over a darker base coat. Almost any color would work well on a small cabinet like this: blue, green, or terra-cotta would all be suitable. To make the glaze, a little of the base color was mixed with ordinary white latex to make a tinted color, and then this was mixed with an equal quantity of acrylic or latex glaze. The glaze was then literally scrubbed over the base color with a paint-brush to build up a mottled surface.

The stamp was cut from a piece of foam and secured to the printing block with contact adhesive. You can use scraps of wood or composite board for the printing block, but make sure it is at least ½ inch (12mm) thick so that it can be held firmly at the sides. Once the printed motifs were dry, the whole unit was protected with pickling wax, which has the added decorative benefit of lightening the paintwork.

MATERIALS

- Cabinet
- White latex primer
- Mid-yellow latex paint
- Cream latex paint
- Acrylic scumble glaze (see page 12)
- Stamping motif (see page 141)
- Contact adhesive
- Gray acrylic color
- Pickling wax

EQUIPMENT

- Household paintbrushes, ½ inch (12mm) wide
- Glass jar or paint bucket
- Photocopier
- Foam rubber
- Masking tape
- Cutting mat
- Craft knife
- Saw
- Wood or composite board
- Flexible glue spreader
- Pencil and steel ruler
- Sheet of glass or flat dinner plate
- Fine-grade steel wool
- Soft cloth
- Screwdriver

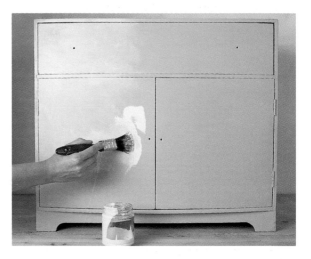

1 Paint the prepared unit first with a coat of white latex primer, then, when dry, with two coats of mid-yellow latex paint. When these, too, are dry, mix an equal quantity of cream latex paint and acrylic glaze in a glass jar or paint bucket. Apply the glaze over the cabinet, moving the paintbrush in a scrubbing motion to build up a cloudy, dappled coat. Photocopy the stamping motif (see page 141) and enlarge it to an appropriate size for the cabinet. Place the photocopy on a piece of foam rubber and secure it in place with strips of masking tape. Place it on a cutting mat to protect your work surface. Carefully cut around the design using a craft knife.

2 Saw a piece of wood to fit the shaped foam. Using a flexible glue spreader, spread contact adhesive on the back of the foam shape and on one surface of the wood block, and let both surfaces dry completely. Then place the two glued surfaces together so that they bond. Contact adhesive only works when two sides of the dry glue are bonded together.

3 When the glaze is dry, mark a panel inside each door of the cabinet using a pencil and a steel ruler. First measure the stamping block and determine the number of stamps that are to be printed in each panel. Subtract the total measurement of the blocks from the measurement of the door, and use this smaller measurement to mark the border.

4 Brush a little gray acrylic color onto a flat surface; I used a sheet of glass, but an old dinner plate is a good alternative. Press the stamping block evenly into the paint, then lift it up. Check that the paint has made contact with the printing surface. Before making the first print, test the block on scrap paper. Use the pencil border lines marked on the door to align the printing block. Press the stamp evenly onto the surface. Then carefully remove the block to reveal the print.

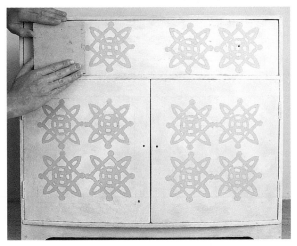

5 Reload the stamp with paint, and continue stamping, taking care to align the stamping block correctly each time. If you get an imperfect print, do not be tempted to reprint. Instead, add any missing details by hand. When the stamped motifs are dry, rub pickling wax into the surface of the cabinet to protect and enhance it. Apply the wax with a pad of fine-grade steel wool, rubbing with a circular motion. Finally, buff the cabinet with a soft cloth, and replace the door handles.

PUNCHED METAL CABINET

This piece of junk was certainly a challenge; it was almost too ghastly to buy. However, the basic framework was sound, the shelves inside were not damaged, and the hinges and door closing were fine. The ugly self-adhesive fake-wood plastic contributed greatly to the cabinet's unsavory appearance, but when this was removed, the piece became a perfect find that was crying out for a complete transformation.

Self-adhesive plastic coverings can be used to disguise any number of flaws on a piece of junk; it is a good idea to peel back a small section if possible to investigate the condition of the underlying surface. Upon close inspection, the door proved to be fine with no visible damage at all. The grooves channeled across it would ordinarily have caused more of a problem, but as the front of the cabinet was going to be covered in aluminum, there was no difficulty.

A cabinet such as this one would usually be used in a bathroom as a medicine chest. However, decorated with a punched metal effect, it is equally suitable in a kitchen, where it can be used for storing herbs and spices.

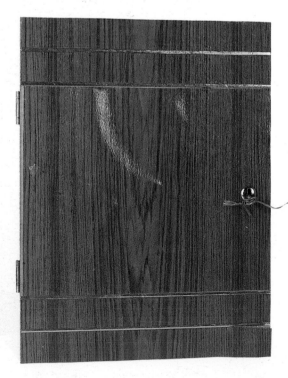

I used a bird motif for the punched tin design, but other designs can also be substituted as you wish. Floral shapes work well, as do geometric patterns and strong heart shapes. Draw your image on a piece of paper first, before committing yourself to the real thing.

This old bathroom cabinet has not only been given a new lease on life, it has also switched roles; no longer used for bathroom bottles and medicines, it is now used for herb and spice storage.

TREATMENT

Once the fake-wood plastic had been pulled away from the door, the cabinet was given a thorough scrub and wash with a strong detergent. The gloss paint that had been painted onto the cabinet was in good condition, with no splits or chips, so I decided simply to "key" the surface with sandpaper rather than stripping back the whole unit. Keying a surface involves scratching an ultra-smooth, painted surface so that the layer of paint subsequently applied has something to stick to. If you apply paint directly onto a glossy surface, it will soon chip off.

The cabinet was then decorated with a sheet of punched metal, which is great fun to do and relatively cheap, too. The metal sheet is not tin, which would be expensive to use, but a thin sheet of aluminum. Most hardware stores should be able to provide you with this type of product. Once the metal sheet is punched with a simple pattern, it is then glued in place on the front of the cabinet with a strong contact adhesive. Additional small, flat-headed tacks are hammered in around the edges of the panel to make sure the tin does not lift up.

MATERIALS
- Cabinet
- Slate blue latex paint
- Sheet of aluminum
- Drawing paper
- Contact adhesive
- Small chrome knob or handle and screw

EQUIPMENT
- Household paintbrush, ½ inch (12mm) wide
- Steel ruler
- Carpenter's square
- Awl
- Tin snips
- Coarse- and medium-grit sandpaper
- Scissors
- Photocopier
- Pencil
- Masking tape
- Hammer
- Flexible glue spreader
- Tacks
- Hacksaw
- Screwdriver

1 Paint the entire cabinet, inside and out, with slate blue latex paint. Measure the front of the cabinet door, using a steel ruler and a square to make sure the angles are accurate. Using an awl, score these dimensions directly onto a sheet of aluminum. Cut out the scored rectangle from the aluminum using tin snips. Smooth the sharp ragged edges of the metal with coarse-grit sandpaper. Then rub both the front and back of the aluminum with medium-grit sandpaper until it is possible to run your fingers along the cut edge. (Take care not to cut yourself when testing the edges.)

2 Trim a sheet of drawing paper to the same size as the aluminum. Photocopy the bird motif (see page 141) onto the paper, enlarging it if necessary, or sketch your own motif if you prefer. Tape the photocopy or sketch over the aluminum. Place it on a work surface and tap out the design with the awl and hammer, making small holes every fraction of an inch.

3 Draw a border around the punched design and tap along this edge using the same punching technique. At first, your progress may be slow, but you will soon find that you develop a rhythm to the punching, and the holes will become more regular and evenly spaced.

4 When the whole design has been punched, slowly peel back the paper to reveal the punched panel underneath. Check the pattern of dots as you do this. If any dots have been missed or there are any gaps in the design or the border, replace the drawing and re-punch the appropriate section.

5 Gently bend the aluminum with your fingers to even out the dents and twists, aiming to get the sheet as flat as possible. Take care when working at the back of the sheet; the punched holes will have sharp edges.

6 Spread contact adhesive liberally over the front of the cabinet door using a rubber-bladed grout spreader or a homemade cardboard spreader. Then spread the adhesive on the wrong side of the punched metal panel in the same way. Let both surfaces dry.

7 Once the glued surfaces are dry, align them carefully, then press them together. Make sure your alignment is accurate, since once the adhesive surfaces touch, they will be difficult to separate. Leave the adhesive to bond for several hours with some heavy books piled on top.

8 When the adhesive has set firmly, hammer in a few tacks along the outer punched edge. If your tacks are slightly too long and the ends push through to the other side, cut them off with a hacksaw.

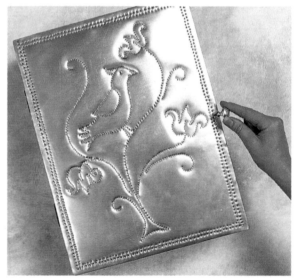

9 Screw a small chrome knob or handle to the front of the cabinet to open and close the door. If you have difficulty finding an appropriate knob, simply spray or gild your own with aluminum metal leaf; if you do this, remember to seal it with polyurethane varnish before attaching it to the cabinet.

THE BEDROOM

Bedroom furniture is readily available from
many junk outlets. Battered blanket chests,
chipped chests of drawers, and dented dressers
are all easily found. In this chapter there are
plenty of creative ideas for improving
shabby junk furniture using techniques such
as stenciling, decoupage, antiquing, and
simple hand-painting.

ANTIQUED CABINET

This attractive cabinet was quite a bargain in a local secondhand store and was simply varnished, so I knew there was little preparation to be done. I didn't worry about the dreadful handles or the formica top as both could be changed very easily. Replacement handles are inexpensive and can greatly alter the character of a piece of furniture. Likewise, formica is easy to paint once the surface has been washed thoroughly and "keyed" lightly with abrasive paper. I particularly liked the simple molding around each of the door panels on the cabinet, which could become an important feature in certain decorating ideas, especially the one I had planned.

I had decided to decorate the cabinet with decoupage and an antiqued, crackle-glazed finish. The decoupage cutouts can be taken from almost any source. I generally use black and white images that I then color softly with watercolors. Colored prints tend to be heavy, and the print tones are too strong for the design to work effectively. Use photocopies to preserve the original prints and use the enlargement facility to scale up the motif according to your piece of furniture. If you use images taken from greeting cards, you will need to peel off some of the cardboard backing before gluing the images in place. Thick card stock will need many layers of varnish applied to get rid of the ridges around

the cutouts; by thinning the card layers behind the image first, you will save time later.

The simple molded details on this bedroom cabinet frame the delicately colored decoupage cutouts perfectly, while the fine cracks of the glaze add to the subtle decorative effect.

TREATMENT

I decided to decorate this bedroom cabinet with tinted decoupage cutouts and an antiqued finish using a crackle varnish, which gives a fine network of cracks over the surface of the cabinet. The crazed appearance occurs when the faster-drying varnish is applied over the slower-drying base varnish. As the cracks are very fine, it is only when they are highlighted with artist's oil paint that the true effect is seen.

A pale green base coat was chosen to show the crackle effect to its best advantage. Note that the application of both the varnish and the oil paint will darken the base color considerably. The motif which was chosen for the applied decoration was taken from a black and white copyright-free source book.

MATERIALS
- Cabinet
- White shellac-based primer
- Pale yellow latex paint
- Decoupage images
- Watercolor or gouache paints
- Pastel fixative or hairspray
- Craft glue
- Water
- Two-part water-based crackle glaze
- Raw umber artist's oil paint
- Mineral spirits
- Polyurethane varnish

EQUIPMENT
- Household paintbrushes, ½ inch (12mm) wide
- Photocopier
- Fine artist's brush
- Small, sharp scissors
- Sponge
- Soft cloths
- Steel ruler
- Pencil

1 Paint the sides of the cabinet, first with white latex primer and then with two coats of pale yellow latex, letting each coat dry before applying the next. Select your decoupage images and photocopy them to the correct size to fit on the cabinet. Using an artist's brush, tint the images with diluted watercolor or gouache paints until you have the right tone. The colors should be muted; test them on a piece of scrap paper first. When the paint has dried, seal the photocopies with pastel fixative or with hairspray. Then cut out the tinted photocopies using a pair of small, sharp scissors.

2 Dilute craft glue in the proportion of one part water to one part glue. Paste the images with this diluted glue, and stick them in position on the cabinet, making sure the edges are stuck down. Using a damp sponge, dab over the surface of the decoupage to remove any air bubbles and excess glue.

3 Apply two-part water-based crackle glaze over the cabinet to produce a delicate cracked finish when dry. Brush on the first part of the varnish using a clean, dry household paintbrush; apply it smoothly and thinly and leave to dry. When the surface is dry, apply the second part of the crackle varnish, again using a clean, dry brush. Apply the varnish as thinly as possible, then leave to dry.

4 When the varnish is completely dry, tiny delicate cracks will have appeared all over the surface. Using a soft cloth, rub raw umber artist's oil paint over the surface of the crackle varnish to highlight the fine cracks.

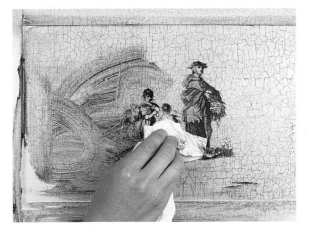

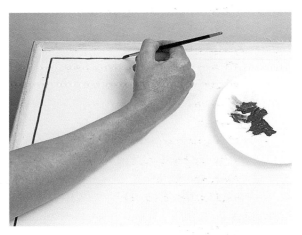

5 Rub off the excess oil paint with a clean cloth; the dark color will remain in the cracks. If there are some areas where there is too much oil paint and it looks too dark, use a little mineral spirits on your cloth to rub it off. The effect should be one of aged cracks; the furniture should not look "muddy" or gloomy. Key the formica surface with sandpaper and prime it with a shellac-based primer.

6 Apply a coat of pale yellow latex paint. Leave to dry. Using a ruler, mark a narrow border around the edge: make small pencil marks 1 inch (2.5cm) from the outer edge, then join them with a pencil line, using a steel ruler. Using a fine artist's brush and raw umber artist's oil paint, paint along the pencil line. Keep the brush evenly loaded with paint to make sure the line retains a regular thickness. When dry, varnish with polyurethane varnish.

DRESSER SET

Mismatched wooden dresser pieces like these can be found in many places and assembled together for a unifying treatment. Here, small candlesticks, a wooden box, and a hand mirror are all treated in a similar way, and they work together perfectly. Other items you might look for could include jewelry boxes and hairbrushes, although the latter should be well scrubbed before decorating. The rich plum base color here was chosen to work with an existing bedroom scheme. Choose your own background color according to your own particular color scheme or simply choose one that appeals. The only colors that should really be avoided are those that are close to the paper cutouts, as the effect will not be as noticeable.

Any shape of paper cutout may be applied over the surface of your junk items. These curly arabesque shapes were inspired by fretwork panels in my own home, but sources can come from anywhere. Printed patterns on fabric or clothes, or patterns from nature could provide the inspiration. Draw or trace your designs on a piece of paper first and shade in the solid areas to gauge for yourself how the final effect will look. Once you are satisfied, you can use it as a template for your design. The fine painted line around the edge of each item gives a neat, crisp finish. Alter this color to match the color of your paper cutouts.

Group together an assortment of mismatched items that would not be out of place on a dresser. Unify these items with a simple decorative treatment such as this unique paper cutout technique.

TREATMENT

These accessories were painted with deep plum-colored latex, and were then decorated with creamy parchment-paper cutouts. Other colors can be selected to match specific decorating schemes, but a deeper color provides a contrast to the paler paper cutouts. Both deep crimson red or royal blue would be suitably dramatic and bold.

The paper cutouts are delicate to handle. I found that it is easier if you apply adhesive to the wooden surface rather than to the paper itself. A successful trick is to dip your index finger in cold water and rub it over the surface of the freshly applied glue; the glue then becomes quite soft, and you will be able to slide the cutout over this surface until it is in the right place.

1 Paint the dresser items with deep plum latex paint and leave to dry. Place the mirror on the parchment paper and draw around the edge with a pencil. Repeat with each dresser item.

MATERIALS

- Dresser items
- Deep plum latex paint
- Semi-transparent parchment paper
- Craft glue
- Water
- Yellow ocher latex paint
- Oil-based varnish

EQUIPMENT

- Household paint-brushes, ½ inch (12mm) and ¼ inch (6mm) wide
- Pencil
- Photocopier
- Cutting mat
- Masking tape
- Craft knife
- Sponge
- Fine artist's brush

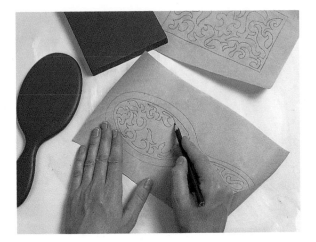

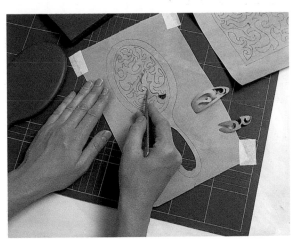

2 Draw a second line approximately ½ inch (12mm) in from the previous line to mark the area that the paper cutout will fill. Draw a decorative design in this central area, either free-hand or photocopy the image on page 140 and transfer it to the paper. Repeat with each item.

3 Lay the parchment paper on a cutting mat and secure with strips of masking tape. Using a sharp craft knife, cut out the decorative image very accurately. Turn the blade smoothly around the corners, keeping the edges sharp.

4 Apply craft glue to the back of the mirror, then stick the paper cutout in position (see Treatment, above). Tap the cutout gently to avoid trapping any air bubbles beneath the paper, which will spoil the effect. Decorate each dresser item in the same way. Dip a clean sponge in water and gently wipe the surface of each cutout to remove any excess glue. Take care not to dislodge the paper; start off by dab-bing downward, and pressing the cutout firmly in place. Leave to dry.

5 Paint a fine line on each of the objects using a fine artist's brush and yellow ocher paint, keeping the line smooth and even. Line the detailing on the turned candlesticks, resting your painting hand on the table and turning the candlestick with your free hand. In the same way, paint a fine line between the cutout image and the edge of the object. Paint oil-based varnish over the cutouts, leaving one coat to dry thoroughly before applying the next. Apply as many layers of varnish as are necessary to smooth out the edges of paper.

BLANKET CHEST

This type of wooden blanket chest should not be difficult to find in your local secondhand store or yard sale. In particular, look out for those boxes with flat sides that have no extra molded decoration, as these will make it easier to create an interesting effect of a gallery of prints, known as print-room, the style of decoration I had decided on for this old blanket chest.

There is a growing interest in print-room decoupage, and you will find no shortage of suppliers of prints. Copyright-free sourcebooks are excellent for reproduction prints and borders. In addition to these, some antique and bric-a-brac fairs have boxes of old prints and engravings that are simple to photocopy. Start to collect an imaginative mixture of prints, perhaps limiting your collection to a single subject or theme, such as architecture or historical buildings. Animal engravings, such as those used here, can create an individual look; botanical images are also easy to source and can look stunning. Black and white images work best; these should be photocopied to preserve the originals. Using a photocopier has the added benefit of allowing you to enlarge or reduce the original to suit your overall design. Other colors that are successful for this print-room style are strong sunny yellow, Wedgwood blue, or creamy off-white.

Use the blanket chest for storing bedroom linens and fabrics or, perhaps more usefully, to resolve the storage problem of books, magazines, or tapes.

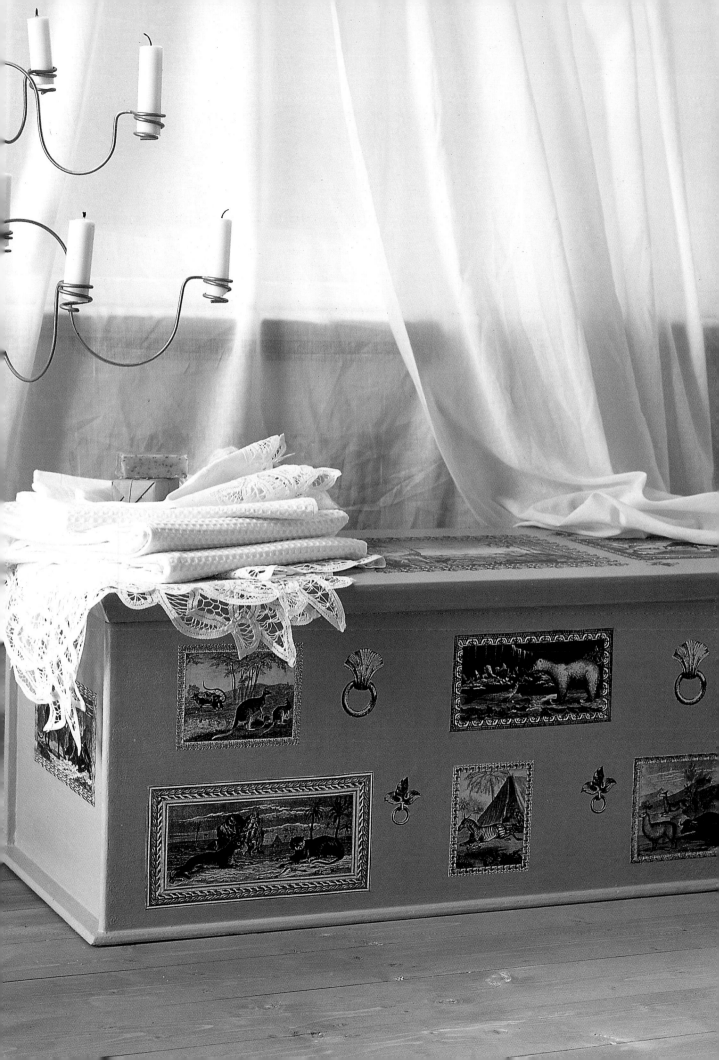

TREATMENT

After preparing the blanket chest, I painted it with a coat of traditional duck's-egg blue paint; but if you prefer, you could use a rich sunny yellow or deep terra-cotta red equally successfully. I then decorated the box with the printed photocopied material, which was glued on in selected positions using diluted craft glue.

Select and assemble all your prints and borders before starting to cut; it is a good idea to make sure that you have extra prints, as you invariably end up using more than you expected. Some print-room styles benefit from being given an antiqued look. One way to do this is to make a cup of strong tea, let it cool, then brush the cold tea over the surface of the prints. Be careful not to saturate the paper; a little tea will work instantly.

Cut out the prints carefully with small sharp scissors and position these on the box using tabs of removable putty where necessary. Next, cut out the photocopied borders. This part of creating the print-room style is usually the most time-consuming. Often the borders are scalloped or delicately shaped, and care should be taken to cut them out neatly. The easiest way to start positioning the prints is first of all to place the largest one in a central position and then to add the smaller ones around it. Then add the scalloped frames, and last the bows or other decorative flourishes.

MATERIALS

- Blanket box
- Duck's-egg blue paint
- Decoupage motifs
- Craft glue
- Water
- Flat oil-based varnish

EQUIPMENT

- Household paintbrush, ½ inch (12mm) wide
- Photocopier
- Pencil
- Small, sharp scissors
- Tape measure (optional)
- Sponge
- Steel ruler
- Craft knife

1 Paint the entire chest with a coat of duck's-egg blue traditional paint, and leave to dry. Select your motifs to decorate the box and photocopy them, increasing the size wherever necessary. I used animal illustrations for the main images and a border print for the framing. Arrange the photocopied images on the box, then mark these positions with faint pencil marks. Vary the sizes of the prints for interest.

2 Cut out all the images and frames using a pair of small, sharp scissors. It is worth spending time doing this neatly, because the more detail you cut out of the framing and decorative pieces, the more effective the whole box will look in the end. Make sure you have enough framing pieces to go around all the images you will be using.

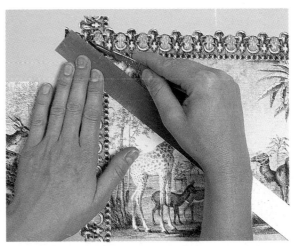

3 Dilute craft glue in the proportion of one part glue to one part water. Brush this glue over the back of each motif in turn, then stick them onto the front of the box using the pencil marks as a guide. Make sure that the images are square with the edges of the box and aligned with each other. Use a tape measure if you are unsure. Wipe off any excess glue with a damp sponge, pushing out toward the edges to remove any air bubbles.

4 Glue the framing pieces in place. To make neat mitered edges, glue the strips of framing so they overlap at the corners. While the glue is still damp, place a steel ruler over each corner in turn at a 45° angle. Cut through the layers of paper with a craft knife. Lift the edges of the framing and peel off the surplus paper. Wipe the surface with a damp sponge. Leave to dry. Then varnish the chest with at least three coats of flat oil-based varnish.

CHEST OF DRAWERS

This chest of drawers was perfect for decorating with a folk-art design. When choosing a piece of furniture to decorate in this style, select one with simple lines and without fussy detailing. This style of decoration would happily suit a larger chest of drawers, but probably nothing smaller unless the scale of the decoration were reduced. Although the painted design is not an authentic representation of some of the wonderful folk-art designs to have come out of North America, it does encapsulate the general ambience of that style of decoration. As traditional folk-art designs often employed leaf motifs, I created a design which used broad oak and ivy leaves twisting around a central stem to form a deep vertical border on each side of the chest.

Sketch your border on a piece of tracing paper, using the motif given on page 138, and joining pieces with tape if necessary. Hold the outline against the furniture to gauge how it will look. If you feel confident to do so, draw in more leaves to extend the border to fit the furniture, if necessary. You may, however, prefer to enlarge the pattern given at the back of the book using a photocopier. Photocopy as many patterns as necessary to make the depth needed to fill your piece of furniture, and then join these together.

Choose a background color that will suit your own decor, but bear in mind that strong, deep colors will work best.

Junk chests of drawers like this can be found in many places and are perfect for a folk-art style of decoration.

TREATMENT

The strong red color of the base coat was given a broken-color treatment using a simple glaze. The semitranslucent color was applied over the dry base coat and was distressed roughly with the bristles of a brush; this effect is more pleasing than that of flat color, and the technique is relatively quick and easy to accomplish. Other colors that could be used for the base coat are deep yellow ocher or burnt orange. Avoid using either blue or green, as the contrast is not strong enough between the base and the leaf colors. Once the base coat was dry, the drawer unit was painted with the decorative twisting leaf pattern.

MATERIALS
- Chest of drawers
- Latex primer
- Dusky pink latex paint
- Plum latex paint
- Latex glaze
- Foliage image (see page 138)
- Dark green latex paint
- Dark plum latex paint
- Black latex paint
- Green latex paint
- White latex paint
- Acrylic varnish

EQUIPMENT
- Household paintbrush, ½ inch (12mm) wide
- Glass jar
- Photocopier
- Carbon paper
- Masking tape
- Pencil
- Fine artist's brush
- Mixing palette or saucer
- Screwdriver

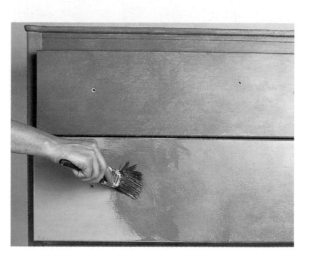

1 Paint the chest of drawers with a coat of latex primer, then a flat coat of dusky pink latex paint and leave to dry. Mix the glaze using equal quantities of plum latex paint and latex glaze. Apply the glaze over the chest by pushing it and gently scrubbing it into the surface with a brush. The pink base layer should be just visible through the plum brush marks.

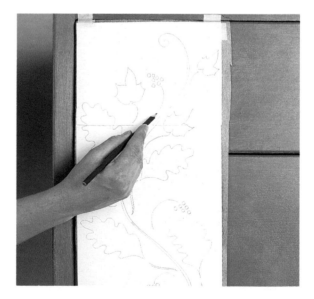

2 Enlarge the foliage image to the right size using a photocopier. Place carbon paper underneath the enlarged image, then secure both to the chest of drawers with strips of masking tape; the inked side of the carbon paper should face the wood. Draw over the lines with a pencil. Reverse the enlarged image and repeat on the other side of the chest.

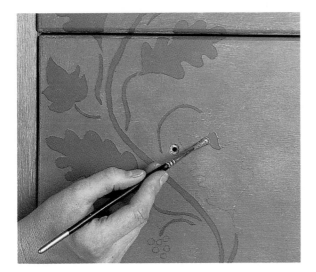

3 Using dark green latex paint and a fine artist's brush, paint the curved stem. Use the same colored paint to fill in the leaves, keeping the paint flat and even. Make sure that the edges of the leaves are neat. It is a good idea to start at the top left-hand corner of the image and gradually work down toward the right, to avoid smudging the paint.

4 Paint the berries individually with dark plum latex paint. When they are dry, mix a darker shade of plum by adding a little black latex paint. Paint a tiny spot of this color on each berry. Leave to dry.

5 Paint details on the leaves in two shades of green to look more realistic. Paint the dark green leaf veins first, to give shape to the leaf, then add the lighter green details. Keep the two kinds of leaf different: the oak leaf has both colors painted throughout, whereas the ivy has dark veins on the left and pale veins on the right, with a line around the edge.

6 Paint pale green highlights on the leaves to give the appearance of light catching the leaves. Always keep the end of the brush pointed when you paint these details to keep the leaves delicate. Leave the decoration to dry, then varnish with acrylic varnish. Replace the drawer knobs to complete the chest.

LINED DRESSER

This piece of junk furniture was a perfect find. As is the case with several of the pieces in this book, it had been abandoned and thrown away, literally junked. It wasn't difficult to see why: an unsympathetic paint finish had been applied over the entire dresser. The end result was several layers of thickly applied gloss paint and oil glaze. I suspect that the thought of having to strip the whole piece back to raw wood again was too daunting a task to contemplate, so out it went.

It is not unusual to find this type of badly painted furniture in secondhand stores and yard sales. Don't be deterred by the surface appearance; paint, no matter how thickly applied, can always be removed. Instead, look at the shape of the piece itself. For me, the proportions of this dresser were particularly attractive. The delicate turned legs had a decidedly elegant appearance, and the arrangement of the four drawers – small drawers on either side of the mirror and two wider drawers under the table top – were beautifully proportioned and created useful storage space. The mirror supports were rather wobbly, but could be fixed by tightening the screws on the hinges. I did notice a little wear and tear that was irreparable – some splitting of the veneer on the drawer fronts – but not enough to dampen my enthusiasm at finding the piece and taking it home.

Despite its rundown appearance, I was struck by the elegant proportions and delicate turned legs of this dresser. To make the most of these features, I have given it a subtle paint and wax treatment, adding lining details to accentuate the furniture's fine shape.

TREATMENT

Once all the hard work of preparing and priming the dresser had been completed (see pages 16–17), I was ready to begin painting. I had decided on a simple treatment of painting and lining, then a final rubbing over with furniture wax for an antiqued finish. When choosing your base color for this technique, always bear in mind that the application of colored furniture wax will alter the final appearance.

The faded and antiqued duck's-egg blue color that now adorns this old dresser started life as a swimming-pool blue that was rather bright, yet if I had started using a color close to the finished look, the pigments in the wax would have masked the delicate tones. Although a professionally lined piece of furniture would be lined by hand using a specialist brush, for our purposes I suggest that you use masking tape for a similar effect. Using this method ensures that all the lines are perfectly even and, more important, perfectly straight.

The first thing to do is to determine where the lines will be and how narrow to

MATERIALS
- Dresser
- Latex primer
- Duck's-egg blue latex paint
- Black acrylic paint
- Antiquing furniture wax

EQUIPMENT
- Household paintbrush, 1 inch (2.5cm) wide
- Steel ruler
- Pencil
- Low-tack masking tape
- Scissors
- Small jar
- Fine artist's brush
- Soft cotton cloth
- Medium-grade steel wool

paint them. On this piece I kept the lining minimal to accentuate the pretty shape of the furniture, confining it to three sides of the table top, the top of the smaller drawers, and the front of the two wider drawers.

1 Remove the drawers from the dresser and work on them separately. Paint the dresser and the drawers with a coat of primer, then a thin coat of duck's-egg blue paint, working it well into any awkward angles. When it is dry, apply a second coat, then leave it to dry again.

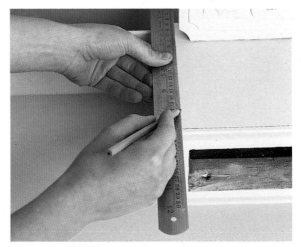

2 To line the three sides of the table top, the top of the smaller drawers, and the front of the two wider drawers, mark the area to be lined. Using a steel ruler and pencil, measure and mark a line ¼ inch (6mm) in from the edge. Then mark a second line ¼ inch (6mm) from this.

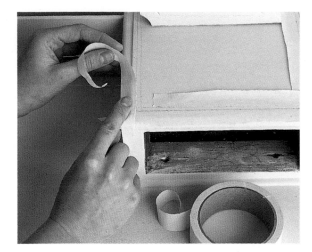

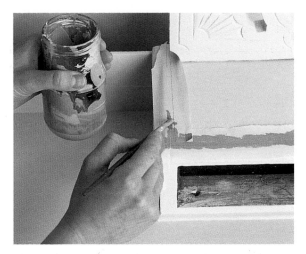

3 Stick low-tack masking tape along the pencil lines to mask the surrounding areas, leaving visible the area to be painted. To reduce the risk of lifting off any paint, burnish down only the edge of the tape nearest to the pencil line and let the rest of the tape remain unstuck. For perfect right angles, cut the tape so it reaches into the corners.

4 To make the lining color, mix a little of the base color paint with a squeeze of black acrylic paint in a small jar. Using a fine artist's brush, apply the paint between the lines of masking tape. Feather the paint inward from both pieces of tape to prevent it from being forced underneath the tape. Remove the tape carefully when you have completed an area.

5 When the lining is completely dry, start to apply the furniture wax. Load a soft cotton cloth with a generous amount of wax and rub it over a workable area of the furniture. You should use enough pressure to make your arm ache after a few minutes. Do not worry if some of the underlying color comes off onto the surface of the cloth; this will enhance the final effect. However, if you start to see the natural color of the wood showing through, rub less hard.

6 Rub a pad of medium-grade steel wool over the surface using a circular scrubbing motion. The aim is to enhance the antiqued finish further and to rub away some areas, as far down as the primed layer. Remove the paint entirely in some places to reveal the natural wood around those edges and corners that would naturally have seen most wear and tear. Soften the lining gently with steel wool to give it a distressed look. Let the wax build up in any nooks and crannies to add to the effect.

SEWING BOX

This charming sewing box was a rather shabby piece of furniture that had been cast aside at a local secondhand store, alongside the equally disastrous-looking bathroom cabinet that was given the punched tin treatment (see page 104). I paid very little for both pieces, and I think I was doing the seller an enormous favor by taking them away. It can be fascinating and often rewarding to scour around at the back of junk stores; in dusty corners, I often unearth the really battered pieces of furniture and more unusual finds that are deemed unsaleable. These can be the most rewarding finds of all, as they are genuine pieces of junk for which people have given up any hope of a future.

I loved the simplicity of this sewing box, and it was perfect for a transformation. The basic structure was sound; there were no wobbly legs, broken sides,

or splitting veneer, and even the hinge mechanism was in perfect working order – it was irresistible. I decided to cover the sewing box with fabric. Almost any printed cotton can be used for this type of decoration. This Toile de Jouy fabric with its picture motif fitted the bill perfectly since the central motif could be positioned on the front, sides, and top of the unit. For covering pieces of furniture with shaped sides, you may prefer to cut a paper template for each section first.

Although this unit could still be used as a sewing box, it makes a rather attractive (if slightly unusual) bedside table. To prevent damage on the top of the unit, cover it with a piece of glass with safely ground edges.

TREATMENT

I had been searching for a piece of furniture that was suitable for covering with fabric, and this sewing box filled the bill in several ways. It had perfectly flat sides with no molding or recessed panels, and a simple flat-fronted drawer. The legs were unfussy with no turned details and, importantly, these were flush with the main top part of the sewing box, which would make fabric-covering it a good deal easier.

If I had chosen to paint the sewing box, I would have had to have undertaken a considerable amount of preparation work. As it was, for the process of covering it with fabric, the unit simply needed a thorough sanding and then a coat of latex primer. As the fabric that I used has a pale cream base color, it was important to work over a pale surface; any dark areas would immediately show through the fabric and spoil the effect. One coat of primer should give you adequate coverage, but if dark patches still show through the layer of paint after one coat, apply subsequent coats until the coverage is even throughout.

I used a Toile de Jouy fabric to cover this sewing box, but other printed fabrics would work just as well. Choose a light cotton fabric, as this is easiest to work with and will not be too bulky at the corners or edges where it needs to be folded over for a neat finish. Silk, satin, gauze, or other delicate fabrics are not suitable for this project as they may mark badly when the glue is applied.

MATERIALS
- Sewing box
- White latex primer
- Light cotton patterned fabric
- Craft glue
- Paper
- Masonite
- Batting
- Plain cotton fabric
- Drawer knob and screw

EQUIPMENT
- Household paint brush, ½ inch (12mm) wide
- Tape measure
- Pencil
- Sharp scissors
- Sharp craft knife
- Tenon saw
- Medium-grit sandpaper
- Screwdriver

1 Paint the sewing box with a coat of white latex primer and leave to dry. If patches of dark color show through the primer, paint on more primer until the color is even. Measure the dimensions of one leg of the sewing box and the length of the leg, allowing a 1-inch (2.5cm) overlap to tuck under the bottom. Transfer these measurements to the wrong side of your chosen fabric, marking the fabric if necessary on the wrong side with a pencil.

2 Cut out the fabric for each leg of the box. Center the printed design of the fabric accurately with the center of each leg, taking into account that the overlap section should be positioned at the back of each leg where it will not be seen. Repeat for the remaining three legs, aligning the print where necessary.

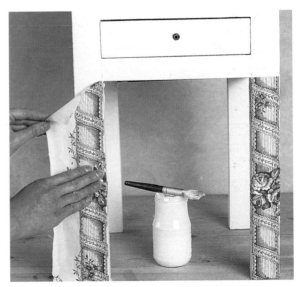

3 Apply a thin coat of craft glue to all surfaces of each leg in turn. Carefully place the fabric in position over the glue, taking care to align the printed design by eye before allowing it to touch the adhesive.

4 When the fabric is positioned, press it down firmly with your fingertips, starting from the center and moving out to avoid trapping air bubbles. A little extra glue may be needed on the overlap.

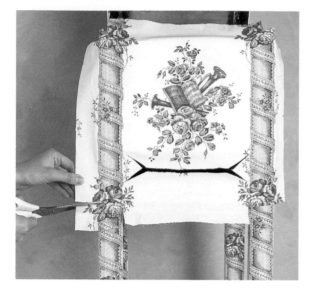

5 Remove the drawer and glue the front section in place. Cut out a hole for the drawer by making a slit across the center of the fabric with sharp scissors; stop 2 inches (5cm) before the edges of the drawer. Then cut diagonally into each of the four corners from this center point. Trim the overhanging edges of the fabric.

6 Glue the flaps down neatly inside the drawer opening, keeping them as flat as possible so that the drawer is still easy to operate. Once the front has been completed, move around the sides of the sewing box.

7 Mark the measurements with a tape measure, and position and glue the fabric over the sides of the box. Apply extra glue at the cut edges to prevent the fabric from fraying.

8 Cover the lid of the box as before, gluing the overlaps neatly inside the lid. Hold the fabric firmly at each corner for a couple of seconds to achieve a neat, flat finish. Use extra glue on the cut edges to hold them securely and to prevent fraying. Although milky when applied, the adhesive will dry to a clear finish.

9 Cover the drawer with one piece of fabric, selecting a piece that aligns with the fabric already in place on the front of the sewing box. Leave the fabric to dry overnight. If the drawer is difficult to slide in, carefully trim away some of the excess fabric from the edges using a sharp craft knife.

10 To pad the inside of the sewing box lid, measure the area to be covered and cut a paper template of this area. Draw this shape on a piece of Masonite and cut it out using a tenon saw. Smooth the rough edges with sandpaper. Cut out a piece of batting using the template and glue this onto the board.

11 Cut out a piece of plain fabric using the template as a guide and allowing an extra 1 inch (2.5cm) all around for turning under. Glue it over the batting; glue the allowance to the wrong side, and let it dry.

12 Glue the padded section in place under the lid. Clamp in place using a wood block to protect both surfaces. Line the inside of the sewing box with the same contrasting fabric as that used for the box lid. Finally, screw a new drawer knob onto the sewing box drawer.

TRACE PATTERNS

Chest of drawers page 124

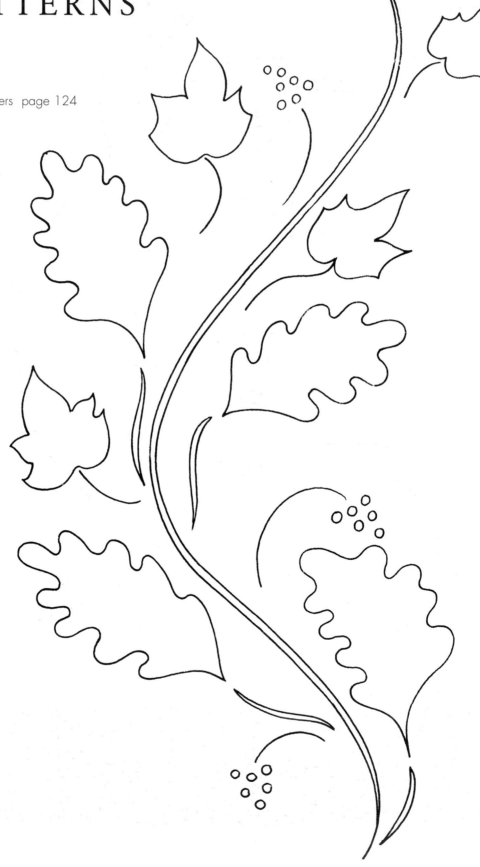

Mosaic table   page 44

Stenciled cabinet   page 40

Kitchen hutch page 92

Damask stenciled chair
page 90

Dresser set page 116

Gilded lamps page 62

Stamped cabinet page 100

Punched metal cabinet page 104

SUPPLIERS

US

Dick Blick Fine Arts Co.
P.O. Box 1267
Galesburg, Il 61402-1267
Tel: 1–800–447–8192
Catalog, artist's paints, speciality and artist's brushes, crackle medium, .005 tooling aluminium, gilding supplies

Pearl Paint
308 Canal Street
New York, NY 10013
Tel: 212–431–7932
(800–221–6845 outside New York)
Catalog, artist's paints, interior paints, glaze mediums and finishes, speciality and artist's brushes, crackle medium, gilding supplies, paint strippers, abrasive papers, pre-cut stencils, mylar, tapes

Janovic Plaza
30–35 Thomson Avenue
Long Island City, NY 11101
Tel: 800–772–4381
No catalog, interior paints, glaze mediums and finishes/varnishes, speciality brushes, crackle medium, gilding supplies, paint strippers, abrasive papers, pre-cut stencils, tapes

Albert Constatine & Sons
2050 Eastchester Road
Bronx, NY 10461
Tel: 800–223–8087
Catalog, finishes/varnishes, gilding supplies, paint strippers, abrasive papers, wood glues, clamps, decorative hardware, clear and tinted antiquing furniture waxes, wood bleaches

Woodworker's Supply, Inc.
5604 Alameda Pl. NE
Albuquerque, NM 87113
Tel: 800–645–9292
Catalog, finishes/varnishes, gilding supplies, paint strippers, abrasive papers, wood glues, clamps, decorative hardware, clear furniture waxes and tinted liming and patinating waxes, wood bleaches

Standard Tile
255 Route 46 West
Totowa, NJ
Tel: 1–800–648–8453
Ceramic mosaic tile, no catalog, will ship anywhere

Canada

Loomis and Toles
1546 Barrington
Halifax, Nova Scotia
B3J 1Z3
Tel: 1–800–565–1545

Omer DeSerres
334 Ste-Catherine Est
Montreal, Quebec
H2X 1L7
Tel: 1–800–363–0318

Omer DeSerres
499 Bank Street
Ottawa, Ontario
K2P 1Z2
Tel: 1–800–677–1820

Loomis and Toles
963 Eglington Avenue East
Toronto, Ontario
M4G 4B5
Tel: 416–423–9300

LewisCraft
1555 Regent Avenue West
Winnipeg, Manitoba
R2C 4J2
Tel: 204–661–8073

LewisCraft
122 Victoria Eaton Centre
Victoria, B.C.
V8W 3M9
Tel: 250–380–9313

INDEX

ACKNOWLEDGMENTS

A special thank you to all those people who were involved in the publication of this book.

To Lucinda Symons for her glorious photography and Jane Forster for her inspiring design work on the book.

Thanks also to Sally for her assistance in simply getting the job done.

Also to the two people who matter most of all, Chris and Jessica.